Creating a Cooperative Learning Center:

An Idea-Book for Homeschooling Families

Katharine Houk

Members of The Alternative Learning Center on the steps of the Morris Memorial building, Chatham, NY.

Katharine Houk

Creating a Cooperative Learning Center

An Idea-Book for Homeschooling Families

Longview Publishing

Creating a Cooperative Learning Center: An Idea-Book for Homeschooling Families

Katharine Houk

Published by: Longview Publishing
29 Kinderhook Street
Chatham, New York 12037, USA
518.392.6900

Copyright © 2000 by Katharine Houk

Cover illustration by Emily Houk
Cover design by WordWorks, East Chatham, NY
Photographs: Paula Lawton – Frontispiece; p.49 – Katharine Houk; p.67– Linda Lyden; p.73 – Katharine Houk; p.79 – Chris Lawton; back cover – Sandy McNay

PUBLISHER'S CATALOGING-IN-PUBLICATION DATA

Houk, Katharine
Creating a cooperative learning center: an idea-book for homeschooling families / Katharine Houk
p. cm.
Includes index.
ISBN: 0-9636096-3-7
1. Homeschooling   l. Title
LC40.H68   2000
372.042--dc21 00-090749

Library of Congress Control Number: 00-090749

Printed in the United States of America

Dedication

To my children — Tahra, Ben and Emily

About the Author

Katharine Houk is co-founder of The Alternative Learning Center, a cooperative which offers classes, workshops, field trips and other adventures for families involved in home education. Her own children began officially homeschooling in 1983.

Katharine lives in Chatham, New York, where she is involved in art (design in fibers), writing, and ministry (interfaith work). She is also director of the Alliance for Parental Involvement in Education (AllPIE), a nonprofit organization dedicated to providing educational information to families.

CONTENTS

Acknowledgements

Introduction
You Can Do It!

Part One: *The Learning Center Story*

Chapter 3

The Nitty Gritty: Organization and Operation   37

Chapter 4

Reflections: The Learning Center & Beyond   97

Part Two: *Processes and Paperwork*

Acknowledgments

This book, like The Alternative Learning Center, is possible because of many people:

• The parents and children who joined with me in the early days to start the original support group, the Home Schoolers' Exchange – and also the many who came from great distances to the meetings in those early years and made it happen.

• Alicia Molinar, who provided the nudge that inspired me to incorporate workshops of the Home Schoolers' Exchange into The Alternative Learning Center.

• Those people who through time have enabled the center to function by continuing and sharing the coordinating work that Alicia and I did at the beginning: Wendy Barnett-Mulligan, Chris Carr, Robin and Greg Denault, Mary Fay, Kaylee Jennings, Beth Lawton, Maura Nedwell, Dede Nerenberg, Tes Reed, Pat and Richard Sahr, Cammy Salazar, and the many others who have helped the center flourish.

• Those who contributed their thoughts, insights and photographs to this book: Wendy Barnett-Mulligan, Chris Carr, Kate Decker, Dorothy Filanowska, Kaylee Jennings, Beth Lawton, Lydia Littlefield, Linda Lyden, Alicia Molinar, Meg Moran, Maura Nedwell, and Mary Ann Schroder.

• Those who supplied support, technical knowledge, proofreading skills, and assistance with publishing details: Jim Cosgrove and Pieter and Sharon Lips.

• Those who gave me the gift of life: Justine Houk, my mother, who listens to me every week, and my father, the late William Houk, who taught me what *radical* means.

• And finally, my partner, steadfast through it all – Seth Rockmuller.

INTRODUCTION

YOU CAN DO IT!

You can do it! You can start a learning center – or resource room – or family cooperative – in your own community. That is the primary message of this book. It is directed to homeschooling families, but the basic ideas presented in it could be used by parents seeking cooperative learning experiences for their pre-schoolers, or during summer months, or by communities when public school systems collapse during the establishment of the new millennium – (just kidding! or am I??....). Although this work was written from a homeschooling perspective and with home educators in mind, it is not a book on how to get started in home education. That topic has been covered well in a variety of places, and there is a list which includes homeschooling resources at the end of this book if you are seeking guidance in that direction.

The family gathering spaces known as learning centers are places that offer educational activities, but they also provide support networks for the people involved in developing and using them. This book is about how such a learning center came into existence, grew, thrived and continues to change. It was written to inspire others to create similar learning alternatives, and it represents my attempt to put into practical and useful form the processes that brought one center into being and have sustained it through time.

On a regular basis I receive phone calls from people saying, "We're thinking of moving to your area because we hear there are great resources there for homeschoolers." My answer is, "Great! Welcome! *But* you don't need to move here. Sprout where you're planted. You can do it yourself, in your own community." Your own community is where you live your day to day life, where you have your roots, where you know your neighbors. There may well already be a learning center functioning near you, or a home education support group or group of parents that's thinking of organizing one. As time goes on I hear about more and more of them.

When my family started homeschooling in the early '80's, there were in our area no support groups, organizations, centers, or events specifically for home educators. The organizations and the center that we have here now were created at the grassroots by the homeschoolers themselves, with no funding from foundations or corporations, no help from other organizations, the state or the local school system. We homeschoolers – ordinary moms and dads – sowed the seeds, and now the entire community is reaping the harvest. If we few could create in our rural area a center which is now a thriving place of learning for over seventy home educated children, you can, too – wherever you live, and however few of you there are. If you build it, they will come.

The phone also rings with calls from people who want help in starting centers of their own. *Creating a Cooperative Learning Center* was created in response to those requests. The book offers a solid and very real example, resources, and ideas (a great variety of ideas!), and will hopefully inspire you. But, as you learn about The Alternative Learning Center (TALC), you will see that it is *not* a program to be precisely followed step by step. It is the story of how one group of people in upstate New

York created an amazing community-based learning alternative which has endured and grown over many years, and which continues to change. You will read about the wonderful things the center offers, but you will also learn about the very real challenges it faces. This book is not utopian, though it does speak of "vision." This account is realistic, containing honest appraisals of short-comings as well as strengths, and tough times as well as good times.

Please also keep in mind that, although the words of others are included in this account, it was put together and given shape by one person – me – with my inevitably limited perspective and biases. Despite this unavoidable and acknowledged limitation, I humbly offer my perspective, hoping that the reader will find something of value in these pages.

Throughout the book and in the Appendices you will find plenty of practical material to help you in drawing up your own paperwork and plans: surveys, bylaws, certificate of incorporation, rules of the center, questionnaires, classes and activities offered, etc. These are included to inspire and inform you, and will need to be reworked and transformed, or totally recreated to meet your own state and local requirements – or even put aside as unnecessary for what you want to do.

Your community will have its unique needs, limitations, and resources, so your learning center's shape will be different than the one I will describe in these pages. It may be a virtual center, held together electronically. It may be organized through a newsletter rather than in a physical space. It may be associated with a school or a public library. It may meet in people's homes, a church or grange, a private school or pre-school, or in public spaces. It may be an independent study program, or a charter school. Possibilities abound!

Our own learning center evolves from one year to the next in its structure, fee scale, number of people served, educational focus, philosophies of those involved, and it has even changed locations several times. Constant re-evaluation takes place. By the time this book is published the center will look different than it does in these pages, as well it should. Change, flexibility, creativity and the diversity of the people involved make up the essence of such a venture, providing the creative tension, challenge and the inspiration that keep it growing and evolving. Your learning center will be unique, as you and your children are unique.

What follows is the book I wish had been available to me back in the early "80's, when I first began dreaming dreams, before my friends and I set out to create what would become The Alternative Learning Center. May you learn from our learning center's experience, and may these tools and suggestions be helpful to you along your way!

Part One:

The Learning Center Story

Chapter 1

Home Education –
The Learning Center's Foundation

Home education is the foundation of the learning center described in this book. As I stated in the Introduction, while the basic ideas presented here could be used by anyone wishing to start a center or cooperative, this book is primarily written for parents whose children of all ages are learning at home and in the world rather than in school.

In this book, I make the following assumptions: 1.) self-direction within the matrix of a varied and supportive environment is essential to deep learning, 2.) the reader has a basic understanding of the many different styles and philosophies of home education, 3.) the reader, as a homeschooling parent, has assumed responsibility for the education of his/her children – and shares that responsibility with the children themselves, and 4.) parents are capable and can be trusted to make wise decisions about their child(ren)'s education, especially when those parents have input and support from others.

continued on page 6

My Children's Story

In the spring of 1983, our daughter Tahra (then 13) was kicked out of school at the end of eighth grade. We were told by the school that "she is not our kind of student." She challenged the authority of her teachers and exhibited other independent behavior and outspokenness which were not appreciated, and thus she was asked to "not return" for ninth grade. This momentous event marked the beginning of our family's home education career and changed our lives forever. At the time I also had an infant and a toddler, Emily and Ben. They, too, have learned at home and in the world, and their first classroom experiences were in college.

When my family started homeschooling many years ago, most people didn't know anyone who was actually doing it, and companies did not produce products and curricula specifically for home educators. Such families were then seen as being on the fringes of acceptability in this culture, as oddballs, fanatics, or "overly protective" parents. In many people's minds home education was considered radical and akin to child abuse. Twenty years ago, people who took their children out of school to teach them at home mostly wanted to be *left alone, which is a natural reaction after turning away from difficult, unmanageable or unresponsive school situations. Because home educators were few and far-between, most families were on their own, whether they wanted to be or not.*

The most precious gift that home education gave our family was time. The children were freed from rigid schedules for learning, and they spent this time in the natural world and with their friends and family. Most important, they enjoyed stretches of solitude – for playing, thinking, daydreaming, reading and imagining, listening to and making music, and delving deeply into the areas of learning that most fascinated them. Their days were structured by the rhythms of family and community life. My spouse and I did our best to provide a rich learning environment, and the children, with our guidance and support, directed their own learning. They learned to read at widely divergent ages (3, 6 and 9 years of age), and throughout we tried hard to remain flexible and responsive to their different learning styles. As they grew older, their learning experiences involved a wider circle of people and became more structured and community-centered. Now they are young adults working and attending college, leading interesting and productive lives.

Although this book was written primarily for home educating families, there is much that teachers and non-homeschooling parents could glean from this book's description of the learning center process. A variety of people from the community have been involved in the learning center. Over the years there has been a mix consisting of parents and their preschool-age children, a few public and private school parents who on occasion removed their children from school for learning center events and classes, homeschooling families, and people from the community who came to share and teach. But this particular center is possible only because the children involved are homeschoolers and therefore have flexible schedules, access to their community's resources and people, and the freedom to do things differently – to recreate education from the ground up. The home education movement is slowly growing up, and the move from an initial "turning away" and individualism to a more inclusive interdependence and community is part of that growth. Homeschoolers, through support groups, conferences, and learning centers, are combining autonomy with connectedness.

While home education was an exciting new adventure in which my own children were obviously thriving, the "individual solution" part of it bothered me. I knew that many children were unhappy in school, or not challenged, or bored, or had needs that were not being met, or had parents who, like me, had goals for their children beyond "global competitiveness." Yet not all parents knew about homeschooling or felt that it was possible for their families, especially if they had to do it "alone." And I myself wanted to connect with other parents on this alternative path.

These realizations fueled my search for people interested in the idea of home education, even if they weren't actually doing it yet (at that time we were the only homeschooling family in our school district). My husband and I traveled to find people, meeting and corresponding with a number of home education advocates, including Nancy Wallace and the late John Holt.

In our own area, I located three forward-looking parents of young children, and together we created a support group called the Home Schoolers' Exchange. People came from great distances to attend meetings because few groups existed in those days. Since then, people from that initial group have started home education support groups in their own areas, which in turn have grown, spawning yet more local groups.

If there isn't a group near you, or if an existing one doesn't seem like the right group for you for one reason or another, start your own. Even if you know only one or two other families who are homeschooling or who have an interest in the idea, that's enough to get started. Check out how people in other areas have gone about starting support groups. You could also advertise in your state's homeschooling newsletter or in your community's local paper. Once you're on your way, you can let local libraries know about the group, and post signs in community centers, churches, and other places frequented by families. Often La Leche League groups, food co-ops, and community-supported agricultural collectives are potential places for finding alternative-minded people interested in home education. And there's always the Internet.

continued on page 10

Starting a Home Education Support Group

People involved in home education tend to be strong-minded, self-sufficient and independent folk, following their own hearts and minds, stepping to that different beat. Many people feel they can get along just fine without belonging to or supporting a group. Why bother? Here are some reasons why.

A support group is:

1. A good place to get accurate up-to-the-minute information about the legalities and regulations involved in home education.

2. A place for parents and children to feel comfortable, to feel a sense of belonging, where they can learn about resources and strategies to help them on their homeschooling path.

3. A vehicle of communication for homeschoolers – through a newsletter and meetings, by means of e-mail, web site, phone tree, or calendar of events.

4. A way to have a voice in creating or revising laws and regulations affecting the lives of homeschoolers.

5. A means of organizing enriching events for parents and children – classes, workshops, field trips, volunteer work, travel, and other learning adventures.

6. A place for personal support! There can be tough times when we need the encouragement and good company of one another, especially if there is conflict with a school official, and also if there is conflict within our own families.

7. A jumping-off point for the creation of a resource center, learning center, or parent-cooperative for homeschoolers.

There has been tremendous growth in the number of homeschooling support groups since the early 80's. There is probably a group near you. Contact a state homeschooling organization to find out. National organizations sometimes have lists, too, but they are not as likely to be as up-to-date as state lists. Attend a homeschooling conference and do some networking. When you have found one or two families, get together and talk while the children play. Discuss and refine what you want to get out of your gatherings; envision the kind of support and resources you would like to have as homeschoolers.

Have a brainstorming session and write your ideas down. They will become your purposes, objectives and goals, and will lead you naturally into deciding how to structure the group in order to meet those objectives. Who will be involved? Both adults and children? Will it be a small informal group or do you want a large and diverse group? Regular meetings? Where? Activities for children? A lending library? Keep in mind that in the beginning you can't do everything at once.

As the group grows, there will be other issues to consider: Will you have membership and dues? A newsletter? An Internet Web site? What if there is conflict; how will decisions be made? Should you have bylaws? Incorporate? Seek tax-exempt status? Who will handle requests for information? What name and address should the group have? What about a bank account? How can the work best be shared so that one person doesn't burn out? (This is *very* important!)

Those of us who have been involved in homeschooling support groups can attest to their value as learning and resource centers in and of themselves. And maybe, since you are reading this book, you can envision a support group leading to the creation of a parent cooperative community learning center.

The first year of meetings, newsletters and networking undertaken by the Home Schoolers' Exchange was exciting and full of possibility. I started organizing workshops for the children each week in my home for the families who belonged to the group. We shared our skills and interests, teaching things ourselves, and sometimes brought in people from the community to teach – or even to entertain. It provided hard-to-find support for both parents and children.

The home education group sponsored many classes, workshops and events, and these group activities were wonderful, but I still dreamed dreams. I envisioned a community gathering place housing resources and voluntary classes led by the children themselves as well as by their parents and other community members. I dreamed of a place that honored the uniqueness of each person while creating vital connections between people of all ages. I longed for a place where homeschoolers could come together for learning and fun – and where others from the community could become involved and see what homeschooling had to offer. I wanted to share with anyone and everyone those things which had worked for us in home education.

The activities, special events and classes which our children enjoyed through the Home Schoolers' Exchange support group eventually "morphed" into The Alternative Learning Center. My dream has come true; in the small town where I live there now exists a cooperative learning center for families involved in home education.

It is my opinion that the learning center vision described in this book offers an example of a form education may take in the future. Many such centers clearly display hallmarks of a possible future shape for education: a re-balancing which emphasizes participation; partnership and cooperation rather than competition; an interdependence which encourages individual growth and maturation; learning through hands-on experience and community work as well as through abstraction; and flexibility and spontaneity rather than fixedness.

We're not just *talking* educational philosophy here; we're *walking* it, too. The exciting part is, the future is *now*! This vision has become real and it's happening. The learning alternative described in this book has been nurtured through many years by a changing stream of dedicated parents and children. This educational gathering place is a living, changing, thriving, (and sometimes struggling) reality; here is the story of how it all began, and how it continues to change and grow.

Chapter 2

Beginnings –
How the Center Was Started

Flashback

It was five minutes before ten on a Wednesday morning. Once again I had left it until the last minute. When my family moved to town after having lived in the country for years, I had rejoiced at the thought that we would be much closer to the learning center, which then was located in the bright and spacious Sunday school area of the local Catholic church. Yet when we lived in the hills and had to drive several miles to the center, we were more likely to be on time because I was more likely to set aside the time for the trip! When we arrived (a couple of minutes late), after parking at the end of the row of cars in the church parking lot and dashing for the door, we found that we hadn't missed the beginning of class.

This particular morning's class was American Sign Language, taught by a mother from the learning center who was a student of sign language herself. Another learning center mom, who had professional experience as an American Sign Language interpreter, helped out with the class as well. My daughter had previously taken sign language at the center, and having enjoyed it immensely, was happy to be taking this follow-up class. On a questionnaire circulated by the learning center she had listed it as one of her favorite classes, along with puppetry. The younger siblings were gathering with their "teacher" for a craft project and stories, and the sign language class for the older children was assembling in an adjacent room. I visited with the other mothers and a father who had brought their children; one of the best things about the learning center is that we parents get to see each other on a regular basis.

• • •

I wrote the above passage a few years ago. Now that the center is well established and offers a smorgasbord of classes, my home educated children are grown, working, and in college. Though my youngest (age 18) and I participated through the center in a "gleaning group" this past autumn (in which adults and children gleaned in farmers' harvested fields and orchards and donated the produce to food pantries and soup kitchens), for the most part my children "aged out" before having a chance to take advantage of many of the newer opportunities the center offers.

I still send in my annual membership, and I drop by and participate when I am able. Because I founded The Alternative Learning Center with friends in 1991, I still feel a strong attachment to it even though many others have taken turns at the helm for some time now. It is a testimony to the importance of its vision that when its founders slowly moved back from roles of major responsibility, others came forward and the center has flourished under ever-changing leadership.

WARNING!

I am about to issue you an invitation, but before I do so I must give you this warning. There is a danger in my putting this fifteen-year process into one book. It is important that the reader realize that the center I am about to describe evolved from just a few families to the many who are now involved. I do hope to inspire you, but at the same time I want to urge you to go slowly, and keep it simple.

Community can't be rushed. As in cooking, too much effort and complexity can obscure the flavors. Too much inspiration or enthusiasm can make for the carelessness of haste. There is value in knowing what not to do, as well as what to do. Start small, and don't try to do it all at once. There. You've been warned. Now...

An Invitation

Are you a parent who for a variety of reasons has been considering home education (or already is homeschooling) but you are concerned about isolation and the socialization of your children? Do you have concerns about helping your children learn things which are enhanced by being experienced in a group, or things with which you may not be familiar, such as foreign languages, or laboratory science?

Have you attended a local support group and joined in their activities, but still wished there was an organized way of getting together more often? Do you wish there was a place for families to get together where parents and children lead classes and workshops on a wide variety of topics? Where people from the community come in to teach, and field trips and opportunities in the community are also part of what the group offers?

The Alternative Learning Center is a community-based family-cooperative gathering place for home educating families, which offers classes, lessons and workshops, group play-time, performances, field trips, a gym, and more for over seventy young people age three and up. Stop by!

An Imaginary Visit

On the day you arrive, outside in the sunshine on the wide steps of the building five or six parents are discussing state testing requirements for homeschoolers while their children are busy indoors. In the lobby of the building you find more parents sitting and talking with one another while small children play nearby. These parents are planning an "astronomy night," when they will meet at one of their homes in the evening to explore the night sky with the older children.

Upstairs you peek in on a French class and a class in which solar cars are being built; in the gym children are involved in cooperative games. Back in the lobby a woman shows you the bulletin board for announcements and items of interest. She also shows you the "mailboxes" – a container of hanging file folders labeled with members' names which people use to communicate with one another.[1] She explains that the center is cooperatively run by parents and children. It all seems too good to be true, and you are eager to become involved.

Several things aren't obvious on your first visit: the slow and uneven process of the center's growth which brought it to where it is today; the ever-changing leadership; the different settings in which the center has functioned and the evolving rules by which it has been run over the years; the dedication, communication, commitment and hard work it takes to keep it running well; and the growing pains the center is experiencing as more and more families with diverse educational philosophies are becoming involved. Here's how it happened.

17

In the Beginning

At the end of the year in 1990 I received a phone call from a parent, Alicia Molinar, who was looking for an educational alternative for her daughters. She and her husband José had explored our area's public and private schools and had considered home education, but were looking for something more. Because I ran a local homeschooling support group and had contacts in alternative education, we were able to call together a group of eight people to discuss educational philosophy and brainstorm ways to make our collective vision real. There was great variety among those original people: one person hankered for a '60's style free school; another was enamored of Montessori education; a third was involved in a Waldorf school but was dissatisfied; a fifth was a public school teacher who was a parent of a very young child, and she wanted an alternative school to be in place by the time her child reached school age.

At our second meeting (ten attended) after much discussion it was decided that the creation of a school was at that time more than the people involved could undertake, considering the time and resources available. However, a learning center had the potential to grow into a school, and could in the meantime be used by people of all ages. I saw the center as a potential place to move the workshops that I had been organizing in my home through the Home Schoolers' Exchange. We parents talked and talked, searching for common goals and recognizing and nurturing each others' strengths. In creating a learning alternative, we were concerned with both individuals' development *and* the development of a strong, cohesive group. We drew out each others' thoughts and potential, fostering the growth of ideas, as we considered a variety of learning approaches and environments. Our anticipation and excitement motivated us, furthering our commitment to the idea of a new, shared, innovative place of learning.

Initial Survey

After much conversation and dialogue with the group, Alicia and I put together an initial survey to ascertain the number of interested families, their geographical locations, and the types of programs and services that interested them. On the next four pages is the survey which our original learning center group put together. If you do a similar survey, the questions in it will be determined by your local needs.

4 April 1991

Dear Parent,

On February 2 and again on February 15, a group of people met for the purpose of discussing the creation of another learning alternative in the Columbia County area. Out of these discussions the consensus was that a learning center would be a valuable addition to the educational alternatives already available in this area. It was decided that the creation of a school would be more than the people involved could undertake at this time, but a learning center has the potential to grow into a school as time goes on. Also, a learning center can be used by families with school children, homeschoolers, and the community in general – people of all ages.

At this time, a learning center is in the planning stages, and in order to more fully assess the needs of families in this area, we are asking for your assistance. It would be very helpful to us to be able to find out if there is interest in a learning center and what services it could provide. We are enclosing a questionnaire; it will be valuable for us if you will fill it out and return it to us. Feel free to share it with other people. Please respond by April 19, 1991.

What types of services would you be interested in?

(Number in order of your priority with #1 as most important.)

_Workshops _Field trips _Theater

_Sports _Art/Crafts _Science

_Learning resources (books, tapes, equipment)

_Referral service to community resources

_Apprenticeship / Mentor Programs

_Clearinghouse for alternative educational information

Please give us your ideas for other services:

How would you use the center?

___As a supplement to school

___As homeschoolers

___As community members

How often would you like the center to be open?

Two or three days a week?

_____

Mornings?   Afternoons?

Evenings?   Weekends? _____

Other suggestions?

How should the center be staffed?

Salaried staff? _____

Parent cooperative? _____

Volunteers? _____

Other suggestions?

How far would you be willing to drive / carpool?

_____ Miles _____ Time (minutes)

Would you like to be involved with the learning center?

_____ In the formation of the center

_____ In using the center for your family

_____ In helping to find financial support for the center

As a teacher___ Volunteer

In donating ___services ___expertise

__materials ___a site for the center

Other ways you might be involved:

Thank you!

Name _____

Address _____

Phone _____

Please return this questionnaire to:

(Here we put the address of one of the members of the planning group.)

Our planning group sent the survey to over one hundred people from the area who had contacted me over the years about education, mostly home educators, but also other community members and people involved with schools. Based on the survey, long range plans included opening the center to school students and adults, but the initial focus centered on home educating families. We drew up draft purposes, decided on a name – The Learning Center – and wrote a press release to send to local papers and homeschooling groups. On pages 28 and 29 you will find the notice that was sent to homeschooling groups for their newsletters.

Purposes and Philosophy

On the facing page is a draft of the purposes and philosophy which was drawn up at a June 1991 meeting in anticipation of writing the bylaws and incorporation papers, which are included in Appendix A in Part Two of this book. By looking at these and other documents you can see how the purposes and philosophy evolved as time went on. Material in parentheses is some alternative language which was being considered at that June meeting.

Purposes

The learning center will provide a place:

- For people of all ages (pre-school through adult) to come together for the purpose of learning in *groups* as well as *individually*;

- With the resources to accommodate people's different learning styles and individual timetables (readiness; progression; rates; schedules);

- For group activities – workshops, tutorials, sports, special events, field trips, etc.

- Where teachers / learners can meet to share what they know, formally or informally;

- For individual research and exploration.

Philosophy

People have a natural desire to learn and make sense of the world. The best learning takes place when participants are given the resources, responsibility, encouragement, and assistance (if and when asked) to pursue their own interests.

Deciding on a name

Our group brainstormed for a name for the center. Just for fun, and to get you thinking, here are the names from our initial brainstorming list:

The Learning Place

Community Resource Center

Our Community Learning Center

The Learning Co-op

Community Learning Co-op

Learning At the Center

A Community Learning Center

The Cooperative

The Family Learning Center

Families Learning Together

Press Release

Shortly after the survey was distributed and results had begun to come in, we realized that we could reach many more home educating families if we contacted support groups in addition to sending the surveys to individuals. Knowing that most of these support groups have newsletters, we sent a press release to area home education groups. This proved to be an excellent way to spread the word.

In 1991, in doing this preliminary research we were limited to what could be sent through the mail; ten years later, some home education support groups have web pages, computer list-serves and on-line bulletin boards. These forums could provide means of quickly and efficiently sending out surveys and notices during your learning center planning process.

The press release we sent to home education support groups is on the next two pages.

New Learning Center Begins to Take Shape

Over the past several months a group of parents from Columbia and Rensselaer Counties has been discussing the establishment of a learning center. The initial participants in the discussions come from a variety of backgrounds – home educators, parents of public school students, and parents of private school students. Various types of programs were discussed, ranging from informally organized workshops to an actual school. As an initial effort, it was decided to focus on a learning center for the upcoming school year.

Once the basic concept of a learning center was settled on, a survey was conducted to ascertain the numbers of families which might be interested in the learning center, their locations, and the types of programs, services, and staffing they would be interested in. Many Home Schoolers' Exchange members participated in that survey, and all others are invited to do so. The initial survey questionnaires which were returned indicate that the Chatham-Ghent area is the geographical center of those who indicated interest, with people from as far away as Massachusetts, Copake, Cairo, and Albany indicating interest. Efforts are now being made to locate a site for the center.

Long range plans include the opening of the center to school students and even adults as well as home educators. However, the initial focus appears to be on a center where home educating families can gather and do projects or workshops together two or three times a week. This has the potential to be a wonderful opportunity for those home educators who are looking for group projects or opportunities for their kids to get together with others. The precise nature of the projects and activities has yet to be decided and will probably depend to a great extent on the interests and wishes of the participants – children and adults.

If you would like more information about the learning center or if you would like a copy of the survey questionnaire to complete, contact: *(Two members of the planning group were listed)*

After considering spaces in churches, libraries, and homes, the group found space in a community center called the Morris Memorial, a large and under-used brick building which at that time provided space two mornings a week for a "parents of pre-schoolers" support group. This space already had toys suitable for young children in one large room, a piano, tables and chairs for adults in another adjoining large room, a small kitchen, and a gym with some equipment. The rent was steep, but we decided to take the plunge and rent the space for three days a week (Tuesday, Thursday and Saturday) for the '91 – '92 school year.

The community center wanted us to have insurance so we purchased a general liability policy. After considerable discussion, we decided that our schedule should include workshops for late weekday afternoons and Saturday as well as during "school hours," so that community members and school children could use the center as well.

Incorporation

For future tax purposes, as well as organizational, continuity and liability purposes, we decided it was good idea to incorporate the center. In New York State, educational non-profits are required to submit paperwork to the State Education Department; one reason is to assure the state that the organization isn't operating a school (which would involve *another* set of requirements). Our carefully worded paperwork passed muster. We had considered a variety of names for the center (see above), ultimately deciding on "The Learning Center," and when we checked, that name was available. This amazed us because it was such a logical choice that we were afraid the name would already have been taken by some other group.

However, when we went back the next day to file the incorporation papers, we found that in the intervening twenty-four hours, some other group had incorporated under the name "The Learning Center," and that particular name was no longer available to us! We hastily added the word "alternative" to the name, went back to the State Education Department and jumped through those hoops all over again, and re-filed the papers with the new name. The process of incorporation cost only about $100, because an attorney had donated his services. This entire process – meeting together, refining our vision, sending out the survey, finding a site, becoming incorporated, getting insurance, sending out publicity – took eight months.

It is also possible to open and run a learning center as a business – a sole proprietorship, a partnership, or a corporation – rather than incorporating as a non-profit. In some states, learning centers are organized as charter schools. In New York, charter school legislation has recently been passed, but such schools are heavily regulated, with mandatory standardized testing. The learning center described in this book chose the non-profit route.

From Co-founder Alicia Molinar

One Step at a Time

As I think about it, what stands out in my mind about starting the learning center is a sense of ease and of everyone working together as a team. Creating a learning center seemed like a reasonable thing, not an overwhelming task. What we all had was enthusiasm and ganas (will) to make something happen. We wanted another educational alternative in our area, and it turned out to be The Alternative Learning Center.

My personal goal for the first meeting was simply to meet the other people who were interested in an educational alternative and to hear what they had to say. We dreamed big dreams that day, each in turn. We weren't hampered by all the things we lacked. That day (and throughout our process) we gave ourselves permission to have it all. A kitchen? Sure thing. A garden? Mmm, yes. A place for group play? Of course. And on and on. We started out with many versions of a place, a school, a center – something we didn't want to name at that point because there were so many possibilities and we didn't want to limit ourselves at such an early point.

Also, it became apparent as we listened to one another that while we all had similar ideas, each of us had a unique *vision. And so we went about shaping the different versions into one. Many of our first meetings were spent in defining a collective vision that would encompass the essence of what we each wanted. And, meeting after meeting, everyone kept coming back. Slowly, the center began to take shape.*

We took one step at a time, letting each day lead us to the next. We discussed everything; we listened to everyone. We set our sights very high as we planned, but we were realistic in our immediate goals. That is, we planned big and started small, leaving ourselves room to grow.

It was the careful attention to the process that made it possible for us to accomplish our goals. We moved with a steady deliberate pace that allowed ample discussion at every step. Concerns were heard and taken into consideration during the planning phase. Since working on the learning center, I have participated in other projects, and it seems that the time we spent in the planning phase and the fact that we didn't pressure ourselves to "finish" helped establish an attitude and spirit of respectful listening and friendly cooperation. The most important thing that we did was to listen to one another. We took the time. In a world that is increasingly in a rush, we took the time to listen, to speak, to ponder. Like the carpenter, we wanted to measure twice and cut once.

continued...

So, what I remember as I put myself back in rural New York, creating a learning center:

- *Beauty, stillness, distance, peace.*
- *Phone calls from my kitchen with the sun shining in.*
- *Katharine, I want a school. Yes Alicia, I too would love a learning center.*
- *Letters, letters, stamps, mail, replies....*
- *Would you be interested? Will you come? Yes, I will.*
- *Driving, driving along the Taconic State Parkway.*
- *Cold nights, ice, snow.*
- *Meetings, meetings, meetings.*
- *Each person a wealth of skills and knowledge. And we used them all.*
- *The family who transported animals. A giraffe at the Howard Johnson's. A wealth of knowledge in our community.*
- *Drinking hot tea. Questions, many questions.*
- *Collating pages. Brochures.*
- *Katharine and I pitching our proposal for the Morris Memorial.*
- *Opening the door to the Morris Memorial and standing in the empty lobby.*
- *We did it!*

The Doors Open

In September 1991, The Alternative Learning Center (TALC) was incorporated as a non-profit organization and opened its doors for workshops three days a week. Our original steering committee, or "Council," had met and assembled a variety of workshops and classes based on brainstorming sessions. In those sessions we came up with classes and skills we wanted to share ourselves, as well as contacts in the wider community who had exciting talents to share (see below). After contacting people and working out a schedule, we printed a simple registration and membership form.

The year was divided into Fall and Spring sessions. To introduce the idea to the community and encourage participation, we did not require membership for attending classes (later on membership was required, as it is at the current time). Copies of the registration form were sent to the people who returned the questionnaire, to home education groups within a forty mile radius, to local schools, public libraries, and other sites where parents might find them. A total of twenty families used the center during the first year; of those, eight became members.

The first year's activities included:
• Writing for Children,
• Experiments with Energy
• The Care and Feeding of Exotic Animals (hence the giraffe at Howard Johnson's!)

- An Introduction to Spanish
- What's in the Doctor's Bag?
- Weaving Workshop
- Halloween Crafts
- Clay Sculpture
- Theater and Dance
- Craft Days
- A Sing-Along
- Making Pop-Ups

There were two field trips to "The Egg" theater in Albany, NY. A list containing a sampling of actual TALC activities that have happened over the past nine years can be found in Appendix C: Smorgasbord.

The center had become a reality!

Notes

[1] See p.68 in Chapter 3 for more about TALC mailboxes.

Field Trip
Mary Ann Schroder

We sat in the auditorium amidst our squirmy, joyful kids. Waiting for the puppet show to begin, I couldn't help but think that belonging to TALC is like having your cake and eating it, too. Without compromising our decision to be in charge of our child's education, we can enjoy the advantages of a group – such as being able to attend "school performances" like this one and having our kids be part of a homeschool peer group. What a great combination!

Chapter 3

The Nitty Gritty: Organization and Operation

The Alternative Learning Center's organization is fluid, defined by the changing needs of the families, the physical location of the center, the number of people involved, the ages of the children, and other factors which continue to change over time. It does have a set of bylaws, but most of its policies, such as parent agreements, have developed and changed over the years. In this chapter and in the Appendices you will find information about these organizational tools and samples of them. The organization of your center will be unique; the example set by The Alternative Learning Center is just one way among many that such a center could be organized. Rather than offering an organizational blueprint, the object of this chapter is to get you thinking about issues that might arise as your center grows and develops.

The days that The Alternative Learning Center is open have changed over time. As you go about deciding how many days to operate a center, you will want to decide how much time you want to put into running it, and balance that with what you want to offer there, while keeping firmly in mind your family's need for time at home and in other activities.

During the first year of the center's operation, one of the workshop days chosen was Saturday because we had envisioned a community center, and wanted all children and families to be involved; we also tried having events late in the day so people could participate after school. For whatever reason, for the most part people beyond the home education community did *not* take advantage of the offerings. Perhaps by the end of the day or week, kids had had enough of being busy with structured "educational" activities and were craving time of their own. School is notorious for gobbling up family time.

As time has gone on, every so often one or another parent has been known to take his or her child out of school temporarily (for a day or a few days) to attend something special at TALC. After the first year the center stopped offering activities on weekends and during after-school time (though now, outside events and classes attended by learning center members do sometimes happen at those times).

After one year at the community center, rent and insurance costs had become prohibitive, and we were not sure we could draw enough families to continue to meet our expenses. At this time Alicia and José Molinar and their family moved to Texas to be closer to their relatives, and Robin and Greg Denault, two other highly involved parents, moved as well. Faced with the daunting task of running the center without these families, I thought maybe I'd give up the public space at the Morris Memorial and move the workshops back into my home.

To my delight, two member moms who believed in the potential of the center stepped up and offered to help: Wendy Barnett-Mulligan and Chris Carr. Together we drew up a questionnaire to help us evaluate the center's first year, to ascertain people's willingness to support the center financially, and to solicit ideas for new workshops and classes.[1] TALC moved temporarily into the homes of two of the members; the center would live on, even if it couldn't be at the community center.

It was very brave and generous of the families that offered to house TALC, and their generosity, coupled with the fact that the center still had a name and an organizing council, served to keep the center going for the Fall '92 session. But the space constraints of the home settings limited the number of things that could simultaneously happen at the center, and after a fall semester in two members' homes, TALC moved to a local church which kindly offered a very nice space for only $25 a month. A few years later, because of renovations at that church, TALC is back at the original community center which it is now able to afford, having grown to serve over seventy children. During this time, TALC's structure, rules and procedures evolved to deal with the growing number of people using the center. The move from the church to the community center involved many changes in policy because of the higher financial costs and because of increased membership and the wider age range of young people using the center. Special meetings were called to deal with budgeting and new policies.

From Dorothy Filanowska

Our involvement with The Alternative Learning Center began with our youngest son's second year of home education, Kelson's third grade if he had been attending school. School had not been a positive experience. Our first year at home, full time together, was a contraction back into our family – a reacquaintance with each other, an affirmation that yes, we could do this home education thing. By the next autumn we were feeling more confident about what we were doing, and ready to reach out for more stimulus and social interaction. So we joined TALC in the fall of 1994, when Kelson was 8 years old, and were active members for three years.

Being a part of TALC was wonderful for us. I'm not sure who benefited more from the experience, Kelson or his parents. Previously, we had been dependent on school for our community and when that was no longer an option, we felt a vacuum that was very painful. TALC provided us with a community. We were certainly a diverse group. I think that for every family that home educates there may be a different philosophy and style, although we share common hopes and dreams for our children. We learned a lot from each other, at those twice weekly work-shops and field trips. Parents shared their skills with the group in workshops, and shared their experiences and ideas and questions with each other during the thousands of impromptu conversations about the daily joys and tri-als of living with children, all of us really caring about how to parent and wanting to do the best job we could. Kelson got to meet and play with a lot of different chil-dren of a variety of ages and participate in workshops and field trips that might never have occurred to us to do on our own.

During our membership at TALC, I witnessed Kelson's growth from a frightened and somewhat angry little boy, to a calmer and confident preteen. When we decided to head off again on our own it was because Kelson's interests had become more specific and he really wanted independence to pursue his own direction and had the confidence to believe in himself.

TALC was an invaluable resource, a loving com-munity, a stimulating and challenging experience – a place where we all learned a little more about our world and lot more about our children and acceptance and our-selves.

Structure and Bylaws

The learning center is not a thing, not a commodity, not even a place. Rather, it is people, ideas, friendship and learning, and above all, it is a relational process. TALC is set up as a parent cooperative. Its purposes, as expressed in its bylaws, are:

"A. To provide a place for people of all ages to share educational resources and knowledge, and to organize and coordinate activities which further such sharing and B. To operate a program of activities for children and youth, using the resources of the community, to encourage learning in its broadest sense."

The people who started the center valued learning that involved deep engagement in the direct experience of things (as opposed to textbook learning), with the all the complexity and multi-dimensionality that such direct experience provides. We aimed for the opposite of a standardized education, building a place where we could guide children in learning from their own experiences, a place where they could formulate and ask questions, experiment, and learn freely and happily. We envisioned the center offering a variety of modes of learning, serving mixed-age groups. The older children would give the younger ones something to aspire to, while the younger ones would remind the older ones of where they used to be. Such groupings also would give the older children an opportunity to share their knowledge. We envisioned a place encouraging creativity, where people of all ages could make things, explore and discover, and through these processes learn self-assessment and self-evaluation. It took a while to discover what structure worked best for such experiential and multi-faceted learning.

The most fundamental concept driving TALC has been its cooperative structure, which involves reciprocity and open-ended mutuality. TALC's bylaws were written after the center had been in operation for awhile. By then we had a stronger understanding of what structure was needed. As it was, several of us had been getting together to plan the programs, and as we drew up the bylaws, we saw no problem with allowing any interested person a place on this organizing council. The more the merrier! All members share in the benefits and the burdens.

We tried to keep the structure very open and flexible so that it could evolve as the group grew. This structure is currently being challenged by the expanding growth of the center; what worked well when the membership was small (about fifteen to twenty families) had become strained as the number of families has grown to well over thirty. This has implications for the center's future structure and direction.

TALC's governing board is called the Council, and any member who is interested can become a council member. This council adopts rules and policies by consensus, plans what will happen at the center, processes registrations, and holds an annual meeting as well as other meetings throughout the year. At planning meetings the upcoming semester's schedule is worked out based on information from workshop/field-trip proposal sheets submitted by each family. There is a rotating coordinator position, as well as secretary and treasurer. In the beginning, the people on the Council who were the most involved and active became the first coordinators.

Now that the center is larger, it is more difficult to get people to come forward as coordinators because the job has become more time-consuming and complex. As home educators we all have families, and time is a precious commodity. Most recently two people have been sharing the coordinator job, and other positions which lighten the load for the coordinators are created as needed.

Over the years, the ways that the parents are involved and the scheduling of classes and events have changed according to the needs of the group. In the beginning the process of deciding what activities to offer and the scheduling was done quite informally. As the number of families involved has grown the center has developed policies which help to keep responsibility more fairly distributed among the families using the center. Otherwise, one or two people end up trying to do everything and quickly burn out. As it is, the coordinators do sometimes feel stressed. The larger and more complex the learning center has become, the more it has needed rules and policies and requirements, especially because it's important that responsibility be distributed fairly. It's a tradeoff: a small group can be more flexible and a large group is more diverse and has more activities to offer. Conflict is inevitable, but conflict can be the catalyst for growth and change. Constant re-evaluation can be tiring, but it is this process which has allowed the center to change and be responsive to needs of its children and families.

Two years into the venture we created the position of Parent Assistant, who was there to open the building, set up, help the person leading the workshop or class, oversee clean-up, and close the building. This job was shared each semester by many parents, and was assigned by the Coordinator (in consultation with the Council). Parent Assistants were notified of their duties with a description put in their registration folders on the opening day of each session. A job description for Parent Assistants, as well as information on a new clean-up policy, may be found in Appendix B in the second part of this book. The Parent Assistant job has evolved and changed over the years as other structures changed and as the center moved from the church to the community center.

Because the families involved are home educating, and at least one parent is usually available during the day, TALC is not a drop-off center. Parents stay and use the time for enrichment and support. If a parent cannot stay, he or she must find an adult present who is willing to be responsible for his or her children that day. The catalyst for this policy was an incident in which a child whose parent was not present was engaging in potentially dangerous behavior; the parent, upon her return, was upset that the child's misbehavior had been addressed in a certain way in her absence. As a result of this incident, the group saw that it was important that each child have someone designated to be responsible for him or her. That's when the *responsible adult* policy was drawn up (see Parent Agreement, p.61). Many of TALC's policies have grown in this way, in response to immediate situations at the center.

Planning the program

In the beginning, the process of deciding which workshops and classes would be offered was done informally at planning meetings. The planning meetings are vital to the center and have become more challenging as the number of involved families has grown. Attendance at these planning meetings has at times been *required* of all members. Questionnaires for both children and adults have been employed to help the planners. Beyond attendance at planning meetings early on in the center's history, there was no set requirement for participation at the center, though parents were strongly encouraged to lead one class or workshop per semester. Because the planning meetings were so important in assuring that everyone's voices and ideas were heard and incorporated into the schedule of offerings, those meetings early on were mandatory for all members. This policy was on-again/off-again, as indicated by the following excerpts from this letter from a TALC coordinator.

46

Dear TALC Members,

When our family joined TALC four years ago the semi-annual planning meetings were mandatory for all members. Upon becoming coordinator of TALC two years ago, I relaxed this requirement and asked that all try to attend, but that attendance would not be mandatory. I have learned that this was a mistake in judgment as our recent planning meeting attendance has fallen to just a handful of members.

This month we will be holding our spring session planning meeting. I am asking that all member families make every possible attempt to be represented at this meeting. If there should be a hardship and this is not possible, then I am asking that you seek another member to present your ideas and speak for you as far as planning possibilities for the spring. The planning meetings of old really were quite exciting to participate in. All members arrived with their workshop sheets in hand and scheduling was done then and there. We all left with a sense of exhilaration and accomplishment in seeing how much could be done when we all contribute. Participating in this meeting also allowed all members a sneak peek at what our next session was shaping up to be. I am hoping that by returning to this old format member families will understand how important their active participation is to the life of a cooperative group.

Thanks so much for your anticipated cooperation in this regard. Keep in mind that we currently occupy our space for a minimum of 50 hours per semester and we attempt to have at least two age groupings of activities ongoing - giving us at the very least 100 planning hours to fill. Ideally, with 30+ member families, a donation of 4 (or more) hours of time per family would go a long way to creating a full and interesting schedule. Should we be fortunate enough to have too many activities, we could create a waiting list of ideas to be used in the event that a scheduled offering is canceled.

Your TALC Coordinator

At the current time, after an initial semester which serves as a grace period during which new members learn how TALC is organized, each family is responsible for one workshop, or event, or class, or series, or field-trip each semester. The families don't necessarily have to lead the class themselves, they can instead find someone from the community, or arrange for a field trip or some other educational experience. Often what is offered is based on what the children have requested. Sometimes the children themselves lead the classes, discovering ways to find out what they want to know how to do, taking the initiative, and sharing their learning with others. In Appendix B you will find an example of TALC's Workshop / Field Trip Proposal Sheets.

The offerings are currently divided by three age categories: 5 and Under, Ages 6-9, and Age 10+. Parents fill out their Workshop/Field Trip Proposal Sheets and give them to three parents (known as age group schedulers or coordinators – not to be confused with the TALC Coordinator) who have volunteered to gather the sheets for each age group and bring them to the planning meeting where the master schedule for each session is put together. At the planning meetings, large sheets of paper with time slots for the days the center is open are taped up on the walls, and using the forms the parents submit, activities are placed on the grid. These activities are then incorporated into the registration form which is sent to members and potential members during the summer. Lately I've been hearing the complaint at the center that there are simply too many wonderful activities to choose from. What a great problem to have!

Ian Bizel and Emily Houk in a TALC performance of
The Water of Life: A Spanish Folktale, *directed by Kate Decker.*

A Teacher's Perspective
Kate Decker

Not more than eighteen months after our family moved to Columbia County, I learned of a few homeschooling families in the area. With a background in education, I was interested in alternative learning approaches. There were plans to form a homeschooling association (TALC) and I was curious to see how this group would take shape. Shortly afterwards, I was asked by Katharine Houk if I would be interested in teaching a theater class for the children of these families. Having studied dance and theater at both the undergraduate and graduate levels, I was eager to lead a creative movement class of The Alternative Learning Center participants.

With my own toddler often accompanying me, I facilitated a series of drama and movement activities in a local community building. The children were always enthusiastic, imaginative in their responses to the material, and accepting of one another. Their receptivity allowed for a deeper level of exploration both in terms of the movement and their developing intellectual capacities. I saw children willing to try new ideas and open to suggestions. Our classes were fun for all involved.

When we moved to the basement of a church in Chatham, the membership of TALC (as it was by then commonly called) grew steadily. The children and I took advantage of the open space there for all sorts of games, warm-ups across the floor, and imaginary journeys. Each six to eight week session of creative movement concluded with an informal presentation of a skit or story which the students chose. Parents, the ever-dedicated audience, were always helpful and supportive, providing everything from refreshments to high-quality costumes.

In any organization, change and growth is a sign of health. Over the past seven years I have seen new families join, course offerings expand (exponentially), and opportunities multiply. The younger siblings of the original group are now filling my classes. It has been highly rewarding to witness the personal growth of all the children I have come to know. A feeling of satisfaction warms me when I see the pre-teens and teenagers take on challenges and succeed in a variety of ways.

As a teacher involved with TALC from its earliest days, I can appreciate the dedication and hard work on the part of the parents which goes into sustaining a group such as this one. I am forever grateful that I have been part of it.

The Strength – and Challenge – of Diversity

Planning meetings have become complex now that TALC is larger and more diverse. Former TALC Coordinator Kaylee Jennings says,

"What an exercise in frustration! Coordinating a group of homeschoolers is akin to getting thirty entrepreneurs to work on a project together."

She suggest that Coordinators need to be blessed with

"1) a true ability to let negativity run off their backs, because no one is ever completely happy with any given semester; 2) a telephone surgically imbedded into their ears (or an ability to let the machine screen their calls and to return all TALC calls at a given time – a tactic that worked for me); 3) fantastic organizational ability; and 4) the patience and humor to get other people to work together for a common goal."

Beth Lawton agrees that diversity is challenging.

"Although we (presently 35 or so families) are not particularly diverse in race or ethnicity, we have a huge variety of educational and parenting/lifestyle approaches and some diversity in socioeconomic background. It is in the area of educational approach that conflict can arise. We range from rather radical unschoolers to folks following the Waldorf school method, to folks utilizing 'store-bought' curricula, to families preferring to use a Christian curriculum – and every possible combination therein (Christian unschoolers, for example).

"All of these folks get together twice a week, with children ranging in age from infancy to early teens. The differences become most obvious during planning times, with some people wanting to offer and include more academically-centered workshops and classes, others wanting to focus on the arts and crafts, and others wishing to utilize TALC more as a recreational and social facility. It takes a creative, patient optimist to pull off each semester's schedule. And the good news is that we have a whole bunch of that kind of folk involved!"

As parents, although we share a desire for nurturing well-educated, sociable, happy children, we each come up with our own theories of child development, based on our children's personalities and behaviors and our experiences in helping them learn. Because families and people are unique, ideas about development and learning can vary quite markedly from one family to the next. Thus some of the offerings at TALC are very structured and class-like; others are more free-flowing and experiential. The people involved try to strike a healthy balance among philosophies of learning. As Beth described, some of the families at the center consider themselves "unschoolers," and have fluid and flexible home educating styles, while others have more structured home education approaches.

For years we home educators have watched and listened as experts in the field of education debate about the best approach to teaching reading, or math, or other subjects, whereas what the learning center embodies is the idea that no single approach is one-size-fits-all, final, or complete. Both children and adults at the center are exposed to many styles of teaching and learning. Each educational experience is held up not as the only way, or the best way, but simply as one possible way. Engaging in learning within such diversity involves learning to live with a certain amount of ambiguity and even risk. Choice can create anxiety, but it also widens our understanding and creates a deeper consciousness regarding possibilities for learning and the many ways learning is best facilitated.

Former TALC coordinator Maura Nedwell agrees with Beth and Kaylee about TALC's greatest challenge and greatest strength.

"TALC's biggest challenge? The biggest challenge TALC has is our vast differences in our membership. We are not a group of like-minded people, and, as such, it is imperative that we respect one another's differences and look beyond them to the common bond that we do share in homeschooling. A lack of respect for, or a discounting of, one particular train of home educating over another causes hurt feelings and divisiveness among our membership, which is a recipe for failure of the whole group.

"TALC's greatest strength? Our greatest strength is our vast differences in membership! We, at TALC, are a melting pot, a microcosm of the world. In coming together as a group, in spite of our differences in opinions, we are offering our children a true glimpse of the world and how to deal with it. For homeschooled children, so often maligned for their lack of 'sociability,' the opportunity that TALC affords to experience a wide array of opinions is invaluable."

Maura's comment that the center is both a melting pot and a microcosm of the world expresses the idea that though we are joined together in working toward a common goal, in that process we retain our particularities and individuality. Not all people who set up cooperatives think that such diversity is desirable.[2] Some feel that the wider the diversity, the less are the chances for developing a workable structure. Some learning centers have admissions policies, regarding philosophical incompatibility as a problem to be avoided. Such centers offer a trial period for new members to determine if the fit is right.[3]

However, diversity is what our children encounter all their lives, and we at TALC have chosen to be inclusive. One of the mothers expressed to me that although she didn't always agree with the child-rearing and educational philosophies of some of the families at the center, she was glad that her child was being exposed to many different ways of being and doing, and she sees the center's diversity as a strength. Diversity can also be a source of ambiguity and tension, but this tension can expand our perspectives, and the ability to live with ambiguity is not a bad thing to possess. The challenge is for this tension between perspectives to become a pathway to deeper understanding, rather than a signal to take sides. The groups that develop within TALC are interdependent; all are needed in order for the center to flourish.

Kaylee Jennings reflects honestly on being a TALC coordinator in the face of such diversity:

"The very nature of homeschooling attracts independent, strong-minded people who all have very specific visions of homeschooling. The more years we each spend homeschooling, the more clear-cut the vision seems to become, making it even harder to form even sub-groups of homogeneous pedagogy. Each of the coordinators that I have gotten to know well has found it to be a rather thankless task that detracts from the time we can spend reaching our own goals, and that trying to move the Learning Center in any one direction is a pointless exercise.

Kaylee continues,

"Everyone, myself included, has gone through a phase of hoping that TALC will be the centerpiece of education and what we provide at home can be the icing on the cake. However, as long as TALC remains an organization embracing many educational philosophies, it can never be 'the cake' to any one family.

"If you look at this problem from another viewpoint, you can see it as providing a wonderful, endless supply of diverse backgrounds. In fact, if anyone should want to attack homeschoolers for sheltering our children in a narrow, rigid world, TALC should more than answer those concerns. In our homogenous little community of Columbia County, TALC represents more diversity of race, religion and philosophy than any other group of thirty families I have ever met. The only real common ground among the thirty is the care for children and concern for their education. These days I think that this is the greatest gift that TALC brings into our lives."

Registration and Opening Day

The center is open two days a week during school hours and field trips are on other days of the week. People register by mail during the summer and again in January using a form that lists all the offerings and their costs, and an activity coordinator/scheduler (the family that planned that class, workshop, or event) is listed for each activity on the registration form (see Appendix E for a sample registration form). On Opening Day families arrive at the center and pick up their registration packets, which contain confirmations of their choices and informs them if they have been placed on waiting lists for particular classes.

Currently, when people send in their registration during the summer, they pay only half the membership and registration fees, and the balance is paid on Opening Day. This saves the treasurer the time and bother of writing out refund checks in small amounts if someone was closed out of a workshop or if a workshop had been canceled for some reason.

The registration packet distributed to each family on Opening Day also contains job assignments, a calendar listing TALC activities for the semester, directions to activities and field trips that are off-site, a families list with names, addresses and phone numbers of member families, and other pertinent information. A class list which has the names of all the people attending that particular class, activity, or field trip, is given to the member who organized that offering (the activity coordinator / scheduler). Communication can then flow directly from class participants to the activity's organizer, thus distributing TALC's work load more evenly among the members. When people have questions about a particular class or activity, it's a tremendous help for them to be able to go right to the activity's originator, rather than to TALC's very busy coordinators.

Agreements and Contracts

Because there are standards of behavior at the center which are expected of parents and young people, agreements were drawn up to be presented to both adults and children for signing on Opening Day. In the words of member Beth Lawton,

> "We often wanted children to follow the rules, and it seemed to me that it was only fair that the rules be presented to them at the onset and in a clear fashion."

As the center grew problems would arise, and sometimes contracts or agreements were developed in response. As a sample, on the following two pages are the Parent Agreement and the Youth Contract which were used in 1994. The use of these agreements and contracts that year resulted, unfortunately, in one family leaving the center. In some ways the learning center mirrors American society's long-standing tension between the interests of individuals and the good of the group. After a couple of semesters the forms no longer seemed to be necessary and the center stopped using them. Family responsibilities are currently explained on the registration form and at orientation meetings for new members.

The Alternative Learning Center
Parent Agreement - 1994

Non-members and Members

• I will honor and agree to help my child honor our few guidelines outlined in the youth contract.
• **Children should not be left unattended.**
• If I am unable to attend a particular field trip or workshop myself, I will designate another specific adult to be responsible for my child that day. I will also notify the parent assistant of any arrangements I have made.
• I will make sure my child understands and feels good about this arrangement.
• I understand that the Learning Center is not responsible for a child left without a designated adult.

Members only

Each member parent will be willing to assist at or facilitate one workshop (effective after the first session of membership).

Parent signature: _____

_____ Member_____ Non-member

The Alternative Learning Center
Youth Contract - 1994

Know your adult (the person who is responsible for you while you are at the center.)
Always let this adult know where you are.

Show respect by being kind...
- to people
- to things
- to furniture

You can expect respect ...
from other children and adults!

Having trouble?
Ask another child or an adult for help.

Remember...
No running, climbing or loud noises and no wandering outside the basement area while you are at the Learning Center.
Leave the center neat.
Everyone helps! That's showing respect!

I understand and agree to follow these rules.

_____

Opening Day, held in September and again for the second session in January or Febuary, is a festive event. Families bring their children and friendships are renewed after the summer months and the winter vacation. Beth Lawton says,

"I got involved in Opening Day activities for the children when I realized that this was their Back to School day and could possibly establish a great attitude for the semester to come. I also had little personal tolerance for the chaos that ensued when the kids all got bored during registration time."

In addition to registration and children's activities, Opening Day also provides exhibit space for local organizations and businesses with educational products or services of interest to TALC's families.

The Alternative Learning Center is a place where individuals' needs and drives are attended to in a communal setting – a place where our children learn to be both self-reliant *and* to share. The structure of TALC consists of multi-layered interactions among people of all ages, where each person is valued, where we work and play, think and do together, where rituals and traditions develop naturally and are preserved, where skills are learned, discoveries are made, and discipline is an expectation, and where we stand accountable to one another – because we altogether are directly responsible for the center's success or failure. It doesn't always work perfectly.

People and Decision-Making

So! In this wonderful process called the learning center, are there ever miscommunications, disappointments, hurt feelings, misunderstandings, impatience and anger, rivalries, disagreements? Does decision-making sometimes become problematic? Of course! After all, people are people.

So far, people have for the most part successfully worked problems through, congeniality has been restored, and folks have grown and expanded their horizons of possibility as a result of this working-through of the people-problems that arise. It's not always easy, especially now that TALC has become so large and diverse. Within the basic consensus process of decision-making, TALC will sometimes decide by consensus to make decisions by vote. Sometimes TALC uses polls written in letter form and sent to members as a way to honor the diversity of responses, for example: "We need to make a decision. Here are our options - A., B., C. – Let us know how you feel about them and tell us if you have other suggestions."

To keep organizational and "people" problems to a minimum, an organization like a learning center needs a structure with clearly defined decision-making processes in place. Currently in TALC, decision-making has been relatively informal, which can become unworkable for a larger group. Because of this informality, over the years the process and commitment related to serving on the Council has become unclear; clarification in this area is essential. Informal changes in the structure as well as policies have been part of TALC's growth process, and, in light of its larger size and increased diversity, TALC is currently beginning to revisit its administrative policies and to firm up its decision-making processes.

Some organizations rely on consensus; others modify this by stating that in the decision-making process, if consensus cannot be reached, a 2/3 majority vote would carry the proposal. Some groups add a "re-vote" option: a re-vote may be called if a new and potentially better suggestion will be proposed.[4] In light of structural changes, it may also be worth considering whether children as well as adults should have voting privileges. Some learning centers have instituted a judicial process for handling disputes and other problems. This process as described by Jane Williams includes children eight years and older on a judicial committee.[5]

What it comes down to is that certain attitudes and behaviors contribute to a better-run organization: the ability to be flexible and go with the flow, the avoidance of clinging desperately to our cherished positions, the opening of our minds and hearts to one another. This requires that we know one another and feel safe with one another. Alicia Molinar described how taking time and really listening is very important in knowing and feeling safe with one another. Some learning places have regularly scheduled therapy-type groups built right into their structure, understanding how important it is for adults to be self-aware and clear in order to be helpful to children and to each other.[6]

Former TALC coordinator Wendy Barnett-Mulligan feels that one reason consensus works well at the learning center is that, because the center serves to augment home education, the group is not dealing with all-or-nothing educational decisions. The depth of the friendships developed at the center plus the strong base of home education upon which the center is built result in the faith that, in some way and in some form, we will always be there for one another. If through some unforseen event the center were to close, Wendy is convinced that the families involved would continue to home educate, and most certainly a new gathering-place would arise. This faith in the continuation of such a place, based on the depths of ties between people and the sense of the value of such a community, combined with the knowledge that home education itself is not threatened by conflicts, makes it easier to reach consensus on daily decisions.

S is for Socialization

For years we in the world of home education have called socialization *the S word.* It's the first word to come to people's lips when they hear that a family is involved in home education. Some homeschoolers share this concern about isolation and look for someplace like a learning center because they want greater opportunities to socialize. Socialization, the ability to get along well and live productively with others, begins at home, and home educated children turn out to be well-socialized even if they never set foot inside a learning center. Some of TALC's families carefully limit their participation in the center's many offerings because they enjoy and value the freedom and natural rhythms of their home and community life with their children. Research studies, my observation of hundreds of homeschooling families, and personal experience have clearly shown me the social success of home education. That said, socialization for both parents and children is an important part of TALC, and it is one reason some home educators join the center. The learning center addresses the isolation that parents of young children sometimes feel by giving adults *and* children opportunities for connection. The place is full of the noise of happy children who have chosen which classes to attend and who look forward to seeing their friends twice (or more) a week. Deep friendships among families have developed, and people often get together for extra outings and off-site activities in the community as a result of the connections they've made at the center.

Owen Barnett-Mulligan and John Lyden
with a crew member, sailing the Clearwater on the Hudson River.

TALC Mailboxes

From a letter by Maura Nedwell, who was TALC coordinator at the time:

We will be starting a NEW SYSTEM.... **TALC MAILBOXES** for all. There have been so many times when I've missed a person I promised information to, or forgotten to see Dede about a check, or wanted to get a group subscription order together – and with the TALC mailboxes, all of these things will be possible and, hopefully, painless!

In the closet there will be a hanging file folder box marked TALC Mail, and each family will have their own mailbox (i.e. hanging folder). If you have a message to pass on, directions for something, a great recipe, etc. you can just put them in the folders for the families you intend. I will also be passing on notes and reminders or information about cancellations, upcoming events, etc. in the same way. Please check your mailboxes whenever you are at TALC.

Outside activities often end up being taken into account when the schedule for TALC's upcoming semester is planned. Members find out about outside opportunities by remaining alert to such opportunities and by placing flyers in TALC mailboxes (see sidebar), notices in the registration packets at Opening Day, or on the TALC bulletin board in the lobby of the building. TALC has published a newsletter off and on, which is also a source of information on activities in the wider community. At present a young person involved in the center is interested in developing a TALC website, which could potentially list community opportunities for fun and learning.

In visiting places of work and taking part in apprenticeships, young people at the center are forging new relationships in the community. Unfortunately, society has become less educationally oriented because school is considered to be the primary location for educational resources. Groups of home educators going on field trips to museums, galleries, zoos, and other community learning facilities are teaching those institutions how to accomodate mixed-age groupings at all hours of the day and times of the week, and thus how to become more responsive to the larger community. Some TALC members think that the center ought to do more toward expansion into the community beyond its walls and make outside gatherings and activities part of TALC as well. In the years ahead, new directions and even a new structure for the center may result from these community interconnections.

A TALC Memory

by Linda Lyden

One of my fondest memories of our TALC experiences is the first Open Stage. The purpose of Open Stage was to allow performers and those interested in performing to present a skill or entertainment to a group of parents and children. After the initial group of performers was done, one child got up to tell a joke. A sense of excitement spread though the crowd as many children remembered jokes and lined up to tell them.

The line was long! Obviously these children were confident and comfortable speaking to an audience, and they had great poise and excellent comic timing. The audience cheered for even the corniest jokes, and the atmosphere in the room was delightful! I was particularly amused to hear a number of bartender jokes. Our family has had many happy TALC experiences since, but that one stands out as particularly memorable.

The nature of home education itself can help to form the social organization of a learning center. When home educators are flexible in what they teach, not sticking to strict grade level requirements, that makes for a learning center with a range of ages in its classes and activities. At home children are encouraged to follow their interests, and at the center children are included in decision-making about what will be offered. Because young people in homeschooling families are intimately involved with their families on a day-to-day basis, often caring for younger siblings or helping with household chores, such behaviors translate into helpfulness in the social institution of the learning center as well. The center exists in the space between private and public life, and is strongly, though not always consciously, built on the idea of a nurturing home.

People at the center form personal bonds and discover new social roles. The children learn to interact with people of all ages, including the young and the old; grandparents and babies are often present. A communal solidarity with its roots in healthy family living is much needed in our culture, where isolation and fragmentation are rampant. The center becomes an outgrowth of the primary ties that families forge at home, knitting our lives together into a satisfying and nurturing whole cloth. A mutuality exists in the learning center "institution." Such mutuality has not become a part of what education looks like in most large school institutions. The center provides a place, in our fragmented world, where children experience a kind of extended family.

For Beth Lawton, the rewards of her involvement with TALC are related to the opportunities TALC provides for learning with others.

"I like that my son has a group of children that he can see on a regular basis and that he can have some of the benefits of group learning and group activities. Although I really don't care if 'other people' approve or not, it certainly quiets *many* detractors of homeschooling when you can say, 'Yes, we belong to a group of forty homeschooling families that meet twice a week.' It shuts 'em right up.

"Personally, I have enjoyed so many things at TALC. Joining when my son was only three, I taught a Colonial History class to a bunch of four and five year old children the next year, and I was delighted by the reality of my dreams of teaching 'across the ages' actually working out with a group of eager children. I loved meeting teenagers who would actually talk to me (an adult) and who were interesting, neat people in their own right. (I think the teenagers were the ones who convinced me to home educate, by the way).

"I have also enjoyed working with a group of pre-teens who wanted to put on a play, attending a History of Jazz class myself, learning how to do many crafts, watching the many performances of Creative Movement and Chorus, and just spending time in a place with other people trying to explore and use the option of home educating their children. This past year, two of us started Homeschooling 101, a weekly drop-in meeting time established in an effort to provide a space for parents to talk about home education, their problems and fears, their successes, resources, etc.; that has also been a satisfying experience for me and it will continue this fall."

Pysanky: Ukrainian Easter Eggs – a class led by Dorothy Filanowska

Often people who feel they have been excluded from exercising power in traditional institutional educational settings, which is sometimes the case with home educating families, assume a deep responsibility when they *do* have that power, as they do in their homeschooling lives and at the learning center. There is an expansive feeling of liberation that comes with the home education decision, and this sense is compounded when people share their new-found vision and experience with others on a similar path.

The extent to which this happens varies; some families are more outgoing and involved than others. Home educators, through support groups and learning centers, can find shared ways of claiming their own voices, and doing it together is a powerful experience. We humans are associative beings.

Generally speaking, we home educators have not deeply considered what the social consequences of our educational choices might mean to institutions. In the early years it was necessary for homeschoolers to define themselves by what they were against, rather than what they were for, and even today I hear the same old *us vs. them* battlefield rhetoric espoused by keynote speakers at home education conferences when they talk about homeschooling versus public schools. One of the effects of the freedom home education offers is that when we are faced with responsibility for our own time and learning, we see how much of our thinking has been reactive. But there is a growing *constructive* sense among homeschoolers, a building up, and a positive picture of what social life and learning communities can be. The friendship, mutuality and interdependence found in cooperative learning centers is sorely needed in our common life. Through their participation at the center, our children are learning to socialize beyond the bonds of family and yet still be the unique people that they are. "Home" is stretching out into the world.

Learning Centers, "Schools," and State Home Education Requirements

Membership at the center as well as activities and classes attended through TALC are regarded by New York State as supplemental to the families' home education efforts. For the most part, TALC provides a wide variety of enrichment activities. Kaylee Jennings expressed her hope that TALC could be the *cake* and homeschooling the *icing*. Maura Nedwell says,

"As my children age, the need for more meat in TALC's offerings becomes apparent, i.e. science labs, music, the arts, and even more sports involvement are the things we seek out."

But some other families do not wish to see TALC become more school-like. Beth Lawton says,

> "The group seems to continue to grow in size (I have introduced motions to limit size but am regularly outvoted), and to be going in a direction that offers more separation by age. In other words, it is feeling more and more like school. Not necessarily a bad thing per se, but it's already been done and I chose not to participate in that particular institution (school)."

These differences in vision may lead to new directions for TALC (see section below on TALC's future). As it now stands, TALC is not a school program or replacement for home education, and individual families are responsible for meeting the state's legal home education requirements. In other states, the interface between learning centers and the laws and regulations regarding home instruction could look different than it does here in New York. In some states (including this one) parents are looking into the possibility of using the charter schools format to support home educators learning together.

At this time, in New York State home educating families are required to submit an annual plan, quarterly reports, and an annual assessment to their local districts. TALC's activities greatly enrich these reports, but the writing of those reports and complying with state requirements is currently up to the parent and child, and is not TALC's responsibility.

Recently I received a call from a mother who was afraid to mention the learning center on her report to her school district. Somehow she thought it might be considered cheating if she as the home educating parent didn't do it all herself. If this parent were relying on a learning center to provide a majority of her child's instruction, then the center would be considered a school under New York State law and she would no longer be considered a home educator.

This, however, is *not* the case with TALC as it is now structured. This state's home instruction regulation does not prohibit homeschoolers from engaging others to help with learning experiences; it simply asks that instructors other than parents/guardians be listed. Even this rule has not been strictly enforced by local districts. On a report, a simple statement indicating that a child attended thus-and-such-a-class at the learning center is entirely appropriate. I encouraged the mother who called me to be honest on her report to her school district, but the amount disclosed to school officials about what happens in a family's home education life is an individual decision each family needs to make.

Beth Lawton says,

"I find great satisfaction in the variety of educational opportunities that are available in our area: public, private, Waldorf, alternative, Sufi, Christian groups, and TALC...there are probably even others I'm not aware of. I like having been instrumental in keeping one of those alternatives alive. There is a good sense of belonging in the group and knowing that others have been served and supported in their homeschooling efforts by our existence."

There have been at least two other learning alternatives which serve homeschoolers in this geographical area: *The Story Center* and *Lifelong Learning Through the Arts*. Descriptions of both programs are included in Appendix F in the second part of this book. They were started by former private school teachers (one of whom was also a homeschooling parent), and both have been more school-like than TALC, with hired teachers and more hours of operation per week.

Because they do not operate as private schools they are free to offer unusual and innovative programs without being subject to the requirements imposed on public and private schools. These learning places function in the area between home education and private schools, and represent another growing phenomenon in the alternative education world.

Display Day

At the end of each semester the center hosts Display Day, a day of high energy, great pride and excitement. As the flyer announcing Display Day proclaimed, "A fun chance to strut your stuff, show your projects, display your writing, bring along grandparents, share a science demonstration, see the results of performing arts classes." The children bring their projects they have done at home as well as projects from classes at TALC, and these are prominently displayed on tables and walls, with posters and photographs. Some projects are even interactive! The drama group presents the play it has been working on, the choruses perform for relatives and friends, and families bring refreshments to share. Reporters from the local press have attended Display Day, at TALC's invitation, and have published their accounts with photographs in local newspapers, thus enhancing the center's visibility in the community.

Valentine's Day crafts for all ages.

Just Another Day at TALC
by Meg Moran

Display Day at the end of our first semester with TALC provided Madeline, then three and a half years old, the occasion for one of her most wonderful and memorable experiences. After participating in the Junior Chorus class and learning most of the songs fairly well, she had become uneasy about chorus as the semester closed when she learned that her group would join the older children's group and perform for parents and other children on Display Day. She didn't think she'd know the song well enough, she didn't want to be with the big kids, and she didn't want an audience to witness her discomfort. Although I assured her that she didn't have to participate, she decided she wanted to practice before Display Day and think about participating. Happily, she did decide to participate, she sang the whole song without hesitation, and she enjoyed herself very much. She was beaming as she sang, and everyone couldn't help but notice her joy and obvious sense of accomplishment.

Of course, many children and their parents have moments like this regardless of how or where they are educated, but this was unique in some respects because of what TALC is. First, my presence and involvement throughout the semester made it possible for me to know the songs she was learning as she was learning them, and our routine of singing them together in a way that helped her learn them was natural and fun and not simply a pre-performance cramming ordeal.

Second, other parents saw Madeline's participation as it evolved – on the outskirts of the class, just watching early on, and then in the midst of the group with enthusiasm later – so they could share her delight, and mine, when she managed, as the youngest of the group, to learn the song and muster the courage to perform. Everything about the occasion was what an uncontrived community experience can and should be. Finally, what struck me at the time and since as particularly heartening is that this was not an extraordinary experience as experiences at TALC go. Madeline's moments of glory on Display Day were a few among many other children's that day and throughout the year, all of them witnessed by and shared with parents, siblings and friends.

Money Matters: Financing a Center

The amount charged per family at The Alternative Learning Center has varied greatly over the years, based on rent and insurance costs and the number of families involved. At first, though we encouraged people to become members, even people who were not members could use the center. Non-members were charged for workshops that were free to members, and they paid a slightly higher amount for workshops which required fees.

There are two semesters, or sessions – September through early December and February through April or May (it varies). Sometimes there is also a summer session, because many people don't like to end all the fun in June! Learning is so deeply a part of living that it can seem nonsensical to limit the center's activities to a schedule based on the public school model. And the warm weather of summer offers possibilities for outdoor activities which are not possible during the "school" year.

Membership for the first year of TALC's operation was $100 per family, or $50 for a half year. In 1992-93, when people met in private homes, the fee was dropped to $50 for the year or $25 for a half-year. In 1996-97 and 1997-98 when the center moved to the church, the cost was $45 for the academic year (September through May). If someone wanted to join in January, they paid $25 for a half-year membership. Currently, with TALC located back at the community center, the membership fee for each semester is $35 per family with a $16 insurance surcharge per child for the year. The membership fee is a charge *per family*, regardless of how many family members participate at the center, while the insurance fee is a charge *per child*. Classes sometimes have extra fees if they require materials or are led by people who wish to be paid. Field trips to performances and museums also sometimes require extra fees. (See Appendix E for a Registration Form that includes costs of the various classes.) All told, the cost for a family of participating in TALC is a small fraction of what a private school education would cost. Even so, finances can present a problem for some families.

In thinking about TALC's challenges, Beth Lawton reflects,

"Another problem issue that comes to mind is the wide disparity in the amount of money that families are willing or able to spend on a learning center. For some of us, who possibly would consider private schooling (with its concomitant tuition), spending a couple hundred dollars a year seems minuscule, particularly in light of the benefits of being in the group. For other families, even fifty or a hundred dollars is a great deal of money and must be justified with clear reasons for spending it and must show an obvious return."

One of the parents for whom TALC's costs are a problem says,

"TALC, in light of all the other activities our children are involved in, is becoming prohibitive in its costs and we are being gradually squeezed out. Granted, 'for pay' classes are wonderful, but multiplied by three and added to the expenses involved in YMCA memberships, soccer, basketball, swim teams, 4-H trips, scouting events, dance classes, hockey clinics, gymnastics, horseback riding, etc. etc. I am starting to weigh the importance of TALC in our lives for the money it costs."

Maura Nedwell, a TALC member and former coordinator, instituted scholarships (called TALCerships) for families needing financial assistance; in exchange for free membership people devote extra energy and time to the running of the center beyond the basic that is required of each family. Funds raised through membership fees are used to pay for rent, insurance, postage and printing, and sometimes for materials. The center operates in the black and has a nest egg for TALCerships and emergencies, and no one, to my knowledge, has ever been turned away for financial reasons.

TALCerships

In exchange for extra help at the learning center, a family can have its membership fee waived. The creation of TALCerships was a way of redistributing the work of the Parent Assistants. In the following excerpt from a July 1997 letter, Maura Nedwell explains the TALCership:

Over the past few years questions regarding our membership fee have come up. We realize that a $45 fee for membership and then the added cost of paying for some individual classes can add up to quite a hefty sum. We are offering a solution for families that find themselves stretched – a TALCership! Frequently in the past we have all agreed that having one person responsible for opening TALC, turning on the heat, lights, remembering how tables are set up, etc. and also locking TALC, turning off the lights, turning down the heat, making sure things are perfect before leaving, would be wonderful.

However, the prospect of paying someone to do this could get sticky. Hence, we are offering the TALCership. If you would like to have free membership, I have blocked off four six-day slots (for four TALCerships) – two slots of six Mondays and two slots of six Wednesdays. To receive free membership, all we ask is that you promise, for the six days assigned, to open and close TALC and be sure that everything is as it should be (I would go over with you all that is required). This would be a tremendous help to our group and would lessen the confusion that sometimes occurs with many people passing on keys and instructions, etc. Please call me if you are interested in this.

Sometimes learning center members discuss the possibility of hiring a coordinator. Up to this point, all the work has been shared cooperatively, and no coordinator has ever been paid for her work at TALC. It is certainly possible to raise more money (either through higher fees, grants, fund-raising, etc.) and hire a director, but TALC has up to this point chosen to keep fees very low and cooperatively share the work load. Recently many of the tasks handled by the coordinators were divided among TALC's members, under the theory that many hands make light work. Both Beth Lawton and Maura Nedwell are concerned about this. Beth remarks,

> "We ran into a conflict in this area in the past year, when the administrative tasks became so large that we discussed hiring a part-time administrator. The group eventually, after many discussions formal and otherwise, voted against hiring, instead creating a series of smaller volunteer positions, each filled by a member. Time will tell whether or not this approach is successful."

Maura says,

> "To have a coordinator deal with the bulk of the responsibilities at TALC was extremely hard on the Coordinator, but protected our membership at large and kept their ideas fresh and enthusiasm levels high, not being drained with administrative worries. Having divided up the Coordinator responsibilities into several

positions (is it eight jobs now?) does truly fulfill the title of 'cooperative' that we profess to be. Yet, tapping so many additional members to handle administrative tasks and still expecting them to contribute chunks of time in teaching and planning for classes may be enough to upset the apple cart. I envision that our members who were gracious enough to take the jobs offered will feel hard-pressed to also offer classes for the children. This opens the door to many more for-pay classes and continues in the direction of making TALC a more exclusive membership. If we are to become more of a resource center than a cooperative, then, why not seek out charter school status and receive funding and allow this prospect to be affordable to all?"

TALC is suffering from growing pains in which financial matters are interwoven with what is being offered at the center and the commitments that homeschooling parents are willing and able to take on. Institutional financial support would be wonderful to have, but always comes with strings attached. It also is difficult to find funders for alternative educational enterprises.

In referring to his efforts to find funding for Pathfinder Learning Center in Massachusetts, Ken Danforth remarks that funders are not eager to support home education and young people leaving public schools.[7] Pathfinder's original proposal for a charter school was turned down, and now that center is supported by tuition ($1500 per year) and fundraisers. A couple of TALC's members have been looking into creating a charter school, and another recently called me about foundation funding she is seeking for TALC's choruses, with the idea of opening the chorus to the larger community. TALC is in transition, and as Beth said, only time will reveal TALC's evolving shape and direction.

Computers and the Internet

The learning center has used the Internet mainly as a communication tool, with members corresponding with one another, submitting newsletter articles to the newsletter editor via e-mail, and receiving the newsletter (in addition to being available by e-mail, hard copy of the newsletter is distributed to TALC members' mailboxes at the center). There have not been classes at the center specifically about using computers or the Internet, though one class (on Antarctica) requested that students have access to the Internet. Once a young member posted a notice on the TALC bulletin board that he was offering classes in computer use to any interested people. Some families are involved on-line individually at home. [As this book went to press, two classes on Internet use, a TALC listserv, and a TALC web page were being planned for the spring semester.]

If someone at the center has a strong interest in learning in cyberspace, the Internet may become more of a factor in the learning center's offerings and/or operation. Perhaps someday TALC will have an Internet web site. Since learning centers are all very different from one another, and in many ways specific to their geographical areas, networking *between* learning centers could be accomplished through the Internet. It could provide a way for geographically distant learning centers to borrow ideas from each other, solve problems together, and support each other in practical ways. Such Internet connections could lead to visits, pen-pals, and family exchanges. Virtual learning centers are also possible, but according to Barbara Humes from the U.S. Department of Education, only about 27% of American homes have computers.[8] I have not seen statistics, if there are any, on how many homeschooling families have computers in their homes.

Regarding the use of computers Gene Lehman says,

"While Internetworking is so seductively intriguing, the most important networking is that which reaches out from each home, through each family, to close neighbors and into helpful communities. Technology can take us into an endless labyrinth of virtually amazing adventures, but it is only through close personal contacts that we *learn about life*. Home and family should provide the strong and steady base that gives us the energy, security and commitment to reach out to others, both near and far, in unlimited, creative, and constructive ways. Next in importance is the community. In general, a home is very much the product of a community, while a community is really no more than an extension of home and family. The ultimate test of any Learning Center is whether it is helping strengthen home and family life and values and serving basic community needs."[9]

Another person recently told me that she was concerned about the use of the computer for learning activities and for interconnection with other people because such activity was all from the neck up. Because computers and the Internet as learning tools are here to stay, it behooves us to know how to use them, but they do not need to become the center of our learning experiences. I can envision places within the community learning center movement for *both* face to face and distance learning; I can also envision learning centers linked with one another to augment and increase the flow of ideas and resources from one to the other, thereby supplementing and complementing what is available to local communities.

What Next?

It is obvious from the above explorations and explanations that although it is indeed a wonderful family resource, The Alternative Learning Center is currently experiencing growing pains. This growth may lead to the search for a larger space, additional days when the center will be open, more off-site classes and experiences, or some other unforeseen reorganization, expansion or division. As stated above, there is also occasional talk of hiring a coordinator to replace the volunteer administrative position which is now shared by TALC's members. Recently people have felt a need to clarify to what extent TALC should be a *buying* cooperative for courses and instructors versus TALC's role as a *parent-teaching* cooperative. Meanwhile, the center is moving toward applying for federal tax-exempt status, which would allow for tax-deductible contributions and greater access to grant money.

While some people are looking into the possibility of setting up a charter school for home educators, others are very concerned about the resultant increased visibility for home education which could lead to increased regulation for all homeschoolers – which, in turn, would diminish the homeschooling movement's valuable ability to pursue innovative and visionary learning practices. Another concern many home educators have is that charter schools in New York State are subject to the same testing requirements as public schools, and testing can drive curriculum and discourage innovation. In other states there may be more flexibility, but generally speaking, with the current nation-wide push for higher standards, laws and regulations governing charter schools are being tightened rather than broadened.

When asked what she thought about TALC's future, Kaylee Jennings said,

> "I wish I had been there in the first two or three years of TALC, because my sense of the group is that it worked much more effortlessly when there were only a few families of very similar educational philosophy with

most of the children closely grouped in age. I'm not sure that TALC is sustainable in its current form because of the administration required to keep it running. As for the future, I think that there will be a growth in homeschooling cooperatives with one main physical facility (like the Morris,* but maybe with more class-rooms and other facilities) run by paid administrators, with several steady instructors for languages, sciences, drama, music and art, overseen by a board of directors that functions much like our council and with families teaching free classes to supplement the more expensive courses run by paid teachers. I do not think that such centers would replace the smaller, more cohesive unit study and subject group cooperatives that are already springing up in the TALC membership, but they would replace the larger cooperative."

Beth Lawton says,

"I must start by saying that anytime anyone asks me about TALC I am filled with a rush of conflicting emotions and thoughts. Great pride that we have ex-isted so long and meant so much to so many children and families; great trepidation that yet another Open-ing Day is looming on the horizon and I will soon have three hours to fill with forty children under my care; great worry about how we will find our way through

* The Morris Memorial Building which currently houses TALC.

the latest in a series of ups and downs in regard to administration and the future direction of the group; and great, sincere commitment to continue with it all, because it truly is worth it in the end.

"I retain an open mind and my greatest hope for the future of TALC is that there are enough other people retaining open minds to find compromises in approach that will enable me to stay involved with the group. Of course, part of the joy of a collective is that it can evolve and grow as the group needs it to. If the resulting shape doesn't fit some of the members' needs, perhaps the home educating community has grown large enough to support two different kinds of collectives. I certainly can see splinter groups that separate happily, with no bad feelings, from the main collective, in order to meet different needs. It is unrealistic to expect TALC to meet everyone's needs, even on a basic level."

The learning center process requires a critical mass of people to survive and succeed, but even just a few families can create a dynamic gathering place. TALC was on the verge of floundering a couple of times early on, but has always survived because of the committed families who are involved. The bylaws are written in a very open-ended way, so that each year the center recreates itself based on what has gone before plus the new and ever-evolving needs of the participants. The center has, however, gradually moved away from some of the processes outlined in the bylaws. It is my hope that the center will revisit the bylaws, making whatever changes are necessary to accomodate the center's needs and structure. [As this book went to press, a bylaws committe had been formed for this purpose.]

Change is the learning center's constant. As a process rather than a thing, TALC looks different from one session to the next, and would look different in different environments. The evolving nature of TALC can be a major source of frustration to those who long to settle on the one *right* way to do it, yet if it becomes ossified, that would lead to a different set of problems.

Some parents feel that TALC has become too large and unwieldy with over seventy children and such widely varying educational needs and visions. Because of this, it is possible that another learning process/entity (or more than one) may soon spin off from the current one. TALC is in labor, and its transition may soon lead to birth!

As the children in TALC get older, members are becoming concerned about their teens and the special needs of older homeschoolers, and are making plans to address those needs, involving the teens themselves in the process. I can easily envision a teen collective being formed by parents and older homeschoolers.[10] A charter school may be another spin-off. Perhaps the center will reorganize into smaller, interconnected TALC nodules. Or maybe it is time for the organization to pull

94

back, reclaiming and refashioning some of its original size, pace and vision. Whatever happens, we would do well to recall Alicia Molinar's words about taking time, listening carefully, thinking big, but taking small steps.

Whatever the future brings, TALC is a shining example of what can happen when people join together to create an educational alternative that is community-based and non-compulsory, and which meets local needs and is flexible and ever-evolving. I see the learning center as a "crucible community,"[11] a place at the living edge of culture where new possibilities are coming into being, through the love and struggle that brings people together for the fulfillment of themselves and their children. As a place that does not coerce learning, it fosters those freely transformative experiences between people that lead to growth and learning. For those who have ears to hear and eyes to see, it offers a vision of what a place of learning can be, and perhaps some of its vision, policies and practices could be incorporated into a radically changed public model. It is my hope that the story of TALC's ongoing process will inspire the start of similar efforts elsewhere.

Notes

[1] See *Appendix B: Day to Day* for examples of questionnaires circulated to the children and their parents.

[2] Linda Koeser and Lori Marse, *The Complete Guide to Successful Co-oping for Homeschooling Families* (Boynton Beach: Self-published, 1995) p. 11. The authors of this Christian-oriented book suggest that all families

in a co-op should have similar homeschooling philosophies. The co-op they advocate consists of groups of children gathering once a month (or more) to be taught a specific lesson by a parent, with parents taking turns.

3 Jane Williams, *Family Learning Cooperatives: Getting Started* (Placerville, CA: Bluestocking Press, 1992) p.5, p.28.

4 I recommend the book *Democracy in Small Groups: Participation, Decision Making and Communication* by John Gastil (Philadelphia: New Society Publishers, 1993)

5 Williams, p.29.

6 The Free School, in Albany, NY is one such place. See the article "A Profile of the Albany Free School" in the magazine *Paths of Learning* (see resources at the end of this book for information about *Paths of Learning*).

7 Neysa C. M. Jensen, "Pathfinder Learning Center: Translating Homeschooling into Community Learning," article in *Home Education Magazine*, September - October 1999, Vol.16#5, pp. 22 - 24. See note 10, below.

8 From *Understanding Information Literacy*, an article by Gene Lehman in the 6/3/99 issue of the newsletter of Learning Unlimited Network of Oregon (LUNO), 31960 SE Chin St., Boring, OR 97009.

9 From *A Learning Center is... Any Space Where Learning Takes Place*, by Gene Lehman, LUNO newsletter 6/3/99. Address above.

10 An example of a program for older homeschoolers is Pathfinder Learning Center, a program started by Joshua Hornick and Kenneth Danford, two former public school teachers. Pathfinder Learning Center, PO Box 804, Amherst, MA 01004.

11 I first learned the term "crucible community" from Larry L. Rasmussen, *Moral Fragments and Moral Community* (Minneapolis: Fortress Press, 1993)

Chapter 4

Reflections:
The Learning Center and Beyond

What we face, friends, are insurmountable opportunities.

Pogo

Home Education Matures

Homeschooling is fostering a gradual revolution[1] in the world of education. For learners to take radical responsibility for their own learning, embedded in family and community, calls for people to change not just in action, but also in heart and mind. When my family first became involved in home education, I felt very much as though we were living on the edge, looking at educational systems from a new perspective and excited about the possibilities inherent in homeschooling, but calling to a basically deaf (or otherwise preoccupied) world.

Now, years later, I have the sense of standing between two epochs, between the times. In joining with others over the years, as home education has become increasingly visible, active, and accepted in the community, I have seen the spinning of connections with the wider world. New forms of cooperation and community are being born. Such communities, which fashion themselves in a trial-and-error way, giving social form to and working out ways of living and learning, just might offer models of learning communities for people on the far side of this educational transition time.

Learning centers can be part of this process of creating connections to the extent that their freedom, energy, activity and power gives freedom, energy, activity and power to others. Our strength is in our ideas, and in our roles as teachers and parents. A few, or even a few hundred, people are unlikely to be heard in the din of state and national educational reform movements. But a single idea, or cluster of ideas, such as those represented by home educators involved in organizing learning communities – if they emerge at the right time and in the right place – can have a major effect. Ideas likely to grow and propagate are emerging at this time from home education group efforts, where people with often widely different educational philosophies and ways of life are engaged in conversation and learning. This grassroots activity demonstrates the power inherent in learning and creating on one's own initiative, and in sharing this process with others.

This learning and sharing through home education and the gathering of learners into centers has been a gradual process, and because it is a human endeavor it harbors the dangers that plague all new social/educational initiatives. Learning centers could be run in insular ways, becoming narrow, protecting special privilege and promoting particular interests. Too great a claim could be made for one particular type of learning center, resulting in standardization and the narrowing of innovative possibilities. They could be limited to the middle class, becoming homogenous life-style enclaves. They could repress minority opinion, considering difference to be deviance. Such problems are one of the major complaints I hear directed toward the idea of the homeschooling learning center as an educational model. People are very used to the public school model of enforcing access and diversity, and have a hard time imagining people being inclusive and open – or even bothering to learn – if they are not forced to do so. This long-standing distrust (fear) of others and what they might do plagues us and stifles innovative approaches to education.

How can people arrive at positions where they are willing to look outward, to change, to risk, to be inclusive, to let go of cherished ideas when letting go is necessary? It only happens if people are not afraid – if they feel safe and supported. Certainly people's basic needs for food and shelter must be met. Beyond the satisfaction of basic needs and the safety provided within the family, the mutuality and community afforded by the relationships developed within a learning center can provide such a safe space. We each need space – psychological and social space, but also a community space in which we are valued for our selves, in which we engage and connect with one another, a space in which we as individuals can make real and concrete choices, and from there participate in the making of social decisions. People who have felt deprived of social (or institutional) space, are rediscovering it through experience in cooperative learning centers.

Learning Care

The freedom involved in homeschooling means families need to make conscious decisions about what learning and education mean to them. Learning can be understood as discovery, involving a mutual and interactive process of engagement with others and the environment. Learning also involves absorbing the best offered by tradition and the experience of those who have come before us. What do we want our children to learn? Facts? Ways of being? Practical wisdom and non-market values are especially important in these times, when people (including our children) are regarded in economic terms and education is seen as preparation for competition in the economic sphere. Certain skills, values and attitudes (beyond memorizing facts and earning money) are taught and learned well in small closely knit groups like families – and cooperative learning centers.

In small-scale groups which function as extended families we learn through imitation, interaction, witnessing, exploring, discovering, and collaborating. Families and small groups temper individualism as a moral way of being and in them people can learn to trust one another. In such cooperative ventures people agree to freely serve, and leadership skills are honed for work together. Together we learn how to deal with the dirty and/or difficult tasks – cleaning up after ourselves, restraining appetites, helping one another. We develop and take part in meaning-giving traditions, learning appropriate social behavior and etiquette, develop qualities of character, practice decision-making, act as models for each other, take responsibility, recover from serious mistakes. Very important, if things should fall apart, we learn to forgive and start anew. In learning all these things in our families and in small cooperative groups, we encounter in microcosm how people engage life in the wider world, and how to find our way in it. One of the reasons that it is easier for such learning to take place in families or cooperative learning centers than in schools is indeed related to the size, but it is also because such centers are *voluntary*. Coercion is not the mode of operation of these voluntary associations.

The moral skills of care for one another learned in small learning center communities have sometimes been extended to create care for people we don't know well (as well as for care of the earth). Through some of TALC's activities people have reached out to the wider community. I think of Marcie Shemaria's gleaning group, mentioned above, which considered the structural causes and social effects of hunger at the same time that it gathered and donated food to area pantries; and the children who worked at soup kitchens, through The Kids Place of Choice, a resource center for home educators on Long Island, NY. The children in both centers also presented plays and performances in local schools, rest homes, and other community organizations. The older children in TALC are considering working as a group for Habitat for Humanity. Such activities are a natural outgrowth of our time spent directing our lives together, engaging in creative activities, achieving common goals, developing our personal and collective agency.

At the heart of the learning center idea is people's responsiveness to one another and to the larger world, born of their desire for the deepest and broadest range of experiences for all involved. At the center we are role models for one another, we have a safe place for exploration, celebration, and support when the going is rough. Beyond offering academics, learning centers play a role in expanding an awareness of what is possible in our lives, and in our children's lives.

Challenges for Parents

Because TALC is a cooperative learning center which requires parent involvement and is not a drop off center, families that don't have that precious resource of time to commit to the center are at a disadvantage. Economic structures and cultural trends in our society work against parents. Families in our culture are under enormous pressures, and in considering the creation of learning alternatives we would do well to consider some of the issues parents face in the raising of children. When we look squarely at the social and economic problems confronting today's families, we come face to face with the basic question of how much the parenting role is valued in our culture, and how our workplaces, economic system, government policies, and popular media value and support - or rather, do NOT value and support, people in their role as parents.

In today's world there is an array of forces working against parents' ability to raise their children well. Economic security is by no means guaranteed, and many government supports for families have eroded in the political climate of the past twenty-five years. Popular culture displays unprecedented materialism and disrespect for persons, as well as outright violence. In the popular media, parents are too often portrayed as stupid, foolish, powerless, and/or irrelevant. Good parenting is undermined by the difficulty of obtaining a living wage, unsupportive communities, parent-bashing in the popular media, government policies that encourage the absence of fathers in the home, and more.

With such powerful systemic, structural forces arrayed against parents and families, what role might home education, and learning centers in particular, play in the struggle for the systemic changes? Some clues can be found in Mary Pipher's book about practical ways troubled families can be helped, *The Shelter of Each Other: Rebuilding Our Families.*[2] She considers the societal forces arrayed against families, but then turns her critical eye to the way helping professionals also undermine family relationships. The book is about how those people who help families can do so in *empowering* ways that don't further create distance and alienation, or undercut the parental role. She is particularly critical of interventions in family life that focus on individual solutions rather than collective well-being.

Pipher bravely uses words like character, will, commitment, and family virtues – words and concepts which need to be reclaimed and transformed from the narrow meanings they are too often given. As her title indicates, she sees a profound need for protection *and* connection. She believes that in our current culture which is in many ways hostile to families, parents must protect the family from what is harmful, and they must find ways to connect outside the family with that which is good and healthy.[3]She believes that solutions must be found "family by family and community by community."

Part three of Pipher's book is called "Solutions," and is of pragmatic value to both parents and others who care about children and want to help them. Her prescription includes helping families with connection, hope, clear thinking, moderation, empathy, humor and creativity. Her list of those things which give families definition, identity, and power are: 1. *Time* – limiting outside activities, turning off the TV, working together. 2. *Places* – homes, sacred places, safe social places. 3. *Interests* – sharing music, gardening, sports, pets. 4. *Celebrations* – anniversaries of special family events, national holidays and invented holidays. 5. *Connecting rituals* – reading together, toasts, visits to relatives, family reunions. 6. *Stories and metaphors* – the "remember whens", metaphors like food (baking and meals together), places – such as kitchens.[4]

These sources of definition, identity, connection and power are not outside the reach of today's families. Family traditions enrich the traditions developed at the center. Home education can give families the gift of time, and learning centers can provide safe social spaces for the sharing of interests, connecting rituals, and shared celebrations and stories. Single parents who wish to pursue home education can be supported through learning centers, which provide centering and orienting forces in a fragmented world.

TALC works against the separation of public and private life, bringing into public spaces those practices which make the home a nurturing place to be. What do we value in our personal and communal lives? How can what we value be integrated into the learning center? These are issues we need to consider as we study and think about the quality of life of our children. What kind of social and institutional structures would best support all parents in the education of their children? Centers like TALC, when they empower people and teach them democratic ways of living and being, have a ripple effect which is felt throughout the community.

Conclusion – A Bright Future

This book's examination of The Alternative Learning Center's history and current situation, in addition to illustrating how a learning center might develop, has provided me an opportunity to explore where TALC has been and where it is going. The center has a great deal already in place upon which to build, and its current growing pains can provide creative forces which push people to develop new ideas that otherwise would not have arisen.

Because people can get so caught up in their busy lives (which at TALC involves the sometimes overwhelming administrative details of running the center), it is difficult to see the bigger picture. The Alternative Learning Center is a rare and important educational experiment, a place that fosters self-knowledge, self-help, and self-control. It awakens, stirs and sets free the imaginations of both adults and children.

Think back on your own education. Remember that special teacher (or maybe more, if you were lucky) who really made an impression on you? Those types of teachers respected you, inspired you and built your confidence. They knew how to draw out those capabilities which lay within you. This process can manifest itself in many different styles of teaching. As parents, we do this drawing out quite naturally with our children because we love them and know them well. The learning center increases our children's chances of meeting up with other teachers and co-learners (of all ages!) who hold the potential of being inspirational for them, because the learning that happens at the center is respectful (based on the interests of learners and teachers), varied (in content and approach) and freely chosen.

The teaching and learning that happens at the center are fun and serious at the same time. The focus of the learning community is centered on concern for the way each individual child is growing. This is the concern and reason-for-being of *any* such center, large or small, urban or rural. We are each contributing to one anothers' successes, and our enthusiasm spills over into the larger community. When people are encouraged through loving interaction to become fully themselves, they are empowered to reach out to and serve others.

As the center evolves, our youngsters are thriving in an exciting and nurturing environment – and if we take the time to step back and look at it, so are we. What an amazing venture a cooperative learning center can be! Our children are growing up as collaborators, sharing resources and knowledge in ways that you and I never were allowed to in the learning environments of our youth. Besides teaching our children academic skills, this learning process enhances a sense of worth and possibility in both adults and children while building within us astrong and tangible sense of our responsibility to others. Our young people, who know how to identify with each other and work together freely, will be likely to carry these skills into working collaboratively to solve problems in the wider world. Seeds are being planted through home education and cooperative learning that have the potential to flower into creativity and social responsibility, making the world a better and kinder place.

I look forward with eager anticipation to two things: 1.) hearing from you, this book's readers, as you nurture and grow learning communities in your own areas, and 2.) witnessing the evolution of TALC, whatever form(s) that may take. Please write to me about your efforts in creating cooperative learning alternatives. Katharine Houk, 29 Kinderhook Street, Chatham, New York, 12037-1215, USA.

Notes

[1] Revolution. A fundamental change in the way of thinking about or visualizing something: a change of paradigm. Definition #2d from *Merriam-Webster's Collegiate Dictionary, Tenth Edition* (Springfield, MA: Merriam-Webster, Inc., 1994)

[2] Mary Pipher, *The Shelter of Each Other: Rebuilding Our Families* (New York: Putnam, 1996)

[3] Ibid., p. 221

[4] Ibid., pp. 230-246

Part Two:

Processes and Paperwork

Appendix A

Organizational Documents

Requirements for incorporation vary from state to state. The documents in this appendix are based on New York State's requiremeents. Included in this section are:

A press release
TALC's Certificate of Incorporation
TALC's Bylaws

Press Release #2

As the center was being formed, an intial press release was sent to homeschooling groups (see pages 28 and 29 in the first part of this book). After the group had decided on a name, the following letter and shorter press release on the next two pages were sent to local newspapers as well as to home education support groups for their newsletters.

The Learning Center
c/o Xxxxxx Xxxxxx
P.O. Box xx
East Chatham, NY 12060

July 2, 1991

Dear Editor:

I am enclosing a press release for a new learning center which is scheduled to open this fall in the Columbia and Rensselaer County area. We would greatly appreciate it if you would include the release in the next edition of your paper or as soon thereafter as you are able.

Thank you for your assistance.

Sincerely,

Xxxxx Xxxxxx
for *The Learning Center*

Announcing: The Learning Center

A group of people from Columbia and Rensselaer Counties are currently planning a learning center. In February, a small group of families met to survey our area's educational needs. As a result of several meetings, The Learning Center is being formed to give our community another educational alternative. Much discussion has centered around the rich, untapped, human resources in the area. The Learning Center would serve as a meeting place to share these resources. For example, potential activities include:

Organizing workshops for children and adults, field trips, individual and small group art and music instruction; planning tutorials; arranging alternative sports activities, children's theater, and special events.

At this time we are continuing our search for a location. Anyone knowing of an appropriate space in the New Lebanon, Chatham, or Hillsdale area, please contact one of the individuals listed below.

For more information, please call *(name & phone number)* or *(name & phone number)*.

CERTIFICATE OF INCORPORATION
of
THE ALTERNATIVE LEARNING CENTER, INC.
Under Section 402
of the Not-for-Profit Corporation Law

The undersigned, natural persons of the age of eighteen years or over, desiring to form a corporation pursuant to the provisions of the Not-for-Profit Corporation Law of the State of New York, hereby certify:

(1) The name of the corporation is **THE ALTERNATIVE LEARNING CENTER, INC.**, hereinafter sometimes called "the Corporation."

(2) The Corporation is a corporation as defined in subparagraph (a)(5) of Section 102 of the Not-for-Profit Corporation Law.

(3) The Corporation is a Type B corporation, as defined in Section 201 of the Not-for-Profit Corporation Law.

(4) The purposes for which the Corporation is formed are as follows:

To provide a place for people of all ages to share educational resources and knowledge, and to organize and coordinate activities which further such sharing.

The Corporation will carry out those purposes by activities such as, but not limited to, establishing a learning center; disseminating information; making referrals; and conducting or assisting others to conduct workshops, seminars, and other educational programs.

Nothing herein shall authorize the Corporation to operate or maintain a nursery school, elementary school, or secondary school.

(5) In furtherance of its corporate purposes, the Corporation shall have the power to solicit charitable contributions and, except as otherwise provided in Article (6) hereof, shall also have all of the general powers enumerated in Section 202 of the Not-for-Profit Corporation Law.

(6) Notwithstanding any other provision of these articles, the Corporation is organized exclusively for educational and charitable purposes, as specified in Section 501(c)(3) of the Internal Revenue Code. The Corporation shall not carry on any activities not permitted to be carried on by a corporation exempt from Federal income tax under Section 501(c)(3) of the Internal Revenue Code or corresponding provisions of any subsequent Federal tax laws, or by a corporation, contributions to which are deductible under Section 170(c)(2) of the Internal Revenue Code or corresponding provisions of any subsequent Federal tax laws.

(7) No part of the net earnings of the Corporation shall inure to the benefit of any member, trustee, director, officer of the Corporation or any private individual (except that the Corporation shall be authorized and empowered to pay reasonable compensation for services rendered to or for the Corporation and to make payments and distributions in furtherance of the purposes set forth in Articles [4], [5], and [6] hereof), and no member, trustee, director, officer of the Corporation or any private individual shall be entitled to share in the distribution of any of the corporate assets on dissolution of the Corporation.

(8) No substantial part of the activities of the Corporation shall be carrying on propaganda, or otherwise attempting to influence legislation (except as otherwise provided by Internal Revenue Code

Section 501[h]), and the Corporation shall not participate in or intervene in (including the publication or distribution of statements) any political campaign on behalf of or in opposition to any candidate for public office.

(9) In the event of dissolution, all of the remaining assets and property of the Corporation shall, after payment of the necessary expenses thereof, be distributed to another organization exempt under Section 501(c)(3) of the Internal Revenue Code, or corresponding provisions of any subsequent Federal tax laws, to the Federal government, or to a State or local government for a public purpose, subject to approval of a Justice of the Supreme Court of the State of New York.

(10) In any taxable year in which the Corporation is a private foundation as described in Section 509(a) of the Internal Revenue Code, the Corporation shall distribute its income for said period at such time and manner as not to subject it to tax under Section 4942 of the Internal Revenue Code; and the Corporation shall not (a) engage in any act of self-dealing as defined in Section 4941(d) of the Internal Revenue Code, (b) retain any excess business holdings as defined in Section 4943(c) of the Internal Revenue Code, (c) make any investments in such manner as to subject the Corporation to tax under Section 4944 of the Internal Revenue Code, or (d) make any taxable expenditures as defined in Section 4945(d) of the Internal Revenue Code or corresponding provisions of any subsequent Federal tax laws.

(11) The office of the Corporation is to be located in the Town of Copake, County of Columbia, State of New York.

(12) The Corporation shall be operated by a board of directors, to be composed of not less than three directors.

(13) The names and post office addresses of the persons to be the Corporation's directors until its organizational meeting are as follows:

NAME   ADDRESS
Xxxxx Xxxxx, W. Street, Ghent, NY 12075
Xxxxx Xxxxxx, S. Road, Copake, NY 12516
Xxxxx Xxxxx, R.D. Box xxx, East Nassau, NY 12062

(14) The Secretary of State is designated as agent of the Corporation upon whom process against it may be served. The post office address to which the Secretary of State shall mail a copy of any process against the Corporation served upon the Secretary is:

Xxxxxxx Xxxxx
 N C Road, Box xxx
East Chatham, NY 12060

IN WITNESS WHEREOF, each of the undersigned incorporators affirms, under the penalties of perjury, that the statements made herein are true. Dated: August X, 1991.

_____
_____

Xxxxx Xxxxxx   Xxxxx Xxxxxx
W. Street, Ghent, NY12075   S. Road, Copake, NY 12516

_____

Xxxxx Xxxxxx

R.D. Box 122, East Nassau, NY 12062

BYLAWS of
THE ALTERNATIVE LEARNING CENTER, INC.

ARTICLE I—PURPOSES

The purposes of The Alternative Learning Center, Inc. (hereafter sometimes referred to as the "Corporation") are as follows:

A. To provide a place for people of all ages to share educational resources and knowledge, and to organize and coordinate activities which further such sharing.

B. To operate a program of activities for children and youth, using the resources of the community, to encourage learning in its broadest sense.

The Corporation will carry out those purposes by activities such as, but not limited to, establishing a learning center; disseminating information; making referrals; and conducting or assisting others to conduct workshops, seminars, and other educational programs.

ARTICLE II—MEMBERS

Section 1: **Eligibility.** Any and all individuals and families may become members of the Corporation.

Section 2: **Definition.** Members of the Corporation shall be those families and individuals who are current in the payment of their membership fees and who have satisfied such other duties and responsibilities as have been set by the Council.

Section 3: **Membership Fee and Responsibilities.** The Council shall set the membership fee and shall determine the time period to be covered by such fee. The Council may also set other duties and responsibilities of membership.

Section 4: **Benefits.** Members shall receive such benefits as may be determined by the Council, including notice of and the opportunity to participate, to the extent that space is available, in the programs of the Corporation.

ARTICLE III—COUNCIL

Section 1: **Number of Council Members.** The Council shall consist of any and all members who choose to serve on the Council.

Section 2: **Term of Council Members.** Each member of the Corporation shall be entitled to serve on the Council for as long as he or she remains a member of the Corporation and desires to serve on the Council.

Section 3: **Powers and Duties.** The Council shall have the general power to manage and control the affairs and the property of the Corporation, including the power to reimburse those incurring expenses on behalf of the Corporation and to authorize the payment of those providing services to the Corporation. The Council shall have the full power, by consensus of those present, to adopt rules and regulations governing the action of the Council. The Council shall ensure that the Corporation adheres to the fundamental and basic purposes of the Corporation, as expressed in the Certificate of Incorporation, as it may from time to time be amended.

Section 4: **Annual Meetings:** There shall be an annual meeting of the Council. The annual meeting shall be held at such place, time, and date as the Council shall designate. Notice of the annual meeting shall be given to all members of the Corporation in a manner likely to provide adequate, actual notice.

Section 5: **Regular Meetings.** Regular meetings of the Council shall be held at such times, dates, and places as may be determined by the Council. Notice of such regular meetings shall be given to all members of the Corporation who have requested in writing that they be given such notice.

Section 6: **Special Meetings.** Special meetings of the Council may be called by any officer or by not less than five members of the Council. Such meetings shall be held at such time, date, and place as may be specified in the notice. Notice of special meetings shall be given to all members of the Corporation who have requested in writing that they be given such notice.

Section 7: **Quorum and Adjournments.** At all meetings of the Council, three members of the Council shall constitute a quorum for the transaction of corporate business. In the absence of a quorum at any meeting, a consensus of the Council members present may adjourn and reschedule the meeting, but otherwise may not conduct any corporate business. Notice of the adjournment and rescheduling shall be given to all members of the Corporation who have requested in writing that they be given such notice.

Section 8: **Organization:** The Coordinator of the Corporation shall preside at all meetings of the Council. In the absence of the Coordinator, those present shall choose a presiding officer. The Secretary of the Corporation shall act as Secretary at all meetings of the Council. In the absence of the Secretary, the presiding officer may appoint any person to act as Secretary at the meeting.

Section 9: **Decision Making.** All decisions of the Council shall be determined by consensus of the Council members present at the meeting, except as otherwise specified in these bylaws or as determined by the Council.

Section 10: **Conflict of Interest.** The Corporation shall enter no contract in which the any Council member or officer has a personal interest, unless such contract has been approved by consensus of the Council members present, provided that no Council member shall vote on a contract in which he or she has a personal interest and the determination of whether consensus exists shall be made as if such Council member were not present.

ARTICLE IV—OFFICERS

Section 1: **Officers.** The officers of the Corporation shall be a Coordinator, a Secretary, and a Treasurer, and may also include such other officers as the Council may elect. One person may hold more than one office in the Corporation, except that a single individual may not serve as both Coordinator and Secretary. The office of coordinator may be held by more than one individual, in which case such individuals shall serve as co-coordinators. Members of the Council may also serve as officers.

Section 2: **Selection and Term of Office.** The officers of the Corporation shall be elected at the annual meeting of the Council. Each officer shall continue in office until his or her successor is elected and qualified, or until he or she dies, is removed or resigns.

Section 3: **Resignation of Officers.** Any officer may resign at any time by giving written notice to either the Coordinator or the Secretary, provided that such notice requirements may not be satisfied by notification to oneself. Such resignation shall become effective not less than thirty days from the date upon which the notice is given. However, the Council, at its discretion, may accept the resignation as effective upon an earlier date stated in such notice.

Section 4: **Removal of Officers.** Any officer may be removed, with or without cause, by the vote of a majority of the Council.

Section 5: **Vacancies.** Any vacancy in any office arising at any time and from any cause (including because of the creation of a new office in the Corporation) may be filled at any meeting of the Council by consensus. Each officer so selected shall hold office for the unexpired portion of the term he or she has been selected to fill.

Section 6: **Coordinator: Powers and Duties.** The Coordinator shall preside at all meetings of the Council of the Corporation. The Coordinator shall have general supervision of the affairs of the Corporation, shall be responsible for the implementation of the various programs and projects of the Corporation, shall keep the Council fully informed, and shall freely consult with the Council concerning the activities of the Corporation. The Coordinator shall have the power to sign alone (unless the Council shall specifically require an additional signature) and in the name of the Corporation all contracts authorized either generally or specifically by the Council. In any situation in which the Coordinator has a personal interest in a contract of the Corporation, the Council shall designate another person to sign in lieu of the Coordinator. The Coordinator shall perform such other duties as shall from time to time be assigned by the Council.

Section 7: **Secretary: Powers and Duties.** The Secretary shall act as Secretary of all of the meetings of the Council at which he or she is present, and shall keep the minutes of all such meetings. The Secretary shall be responsible for giving and serving all notices of the Corporation, and shall perform all the duties incident to the office of Secretary, subject at all times, however, to the control of the Council. The Secretary shall perform such other duties as shall from time to time be assigned to him or her by the Council.

Section 8: **Treasurer: Powers and Duties.** The Treasurer shall have custody of all funds and securities of the Corporation which may come into his or her hands. The Treasurer shall keep (or shall cause to be kept) complete and accurate accounts of the receipts and disbursements of the Corporation, and he or she shall deposit (or shall cause to be deposited) all monies and other valuable effects of the Corporation in the name of and to the credit of the Corporation in such banks and depositories as the Council may designate. Whenever required by the Council, the Treasurer shall render a statement of the Corporation's accounts. Upon reasonable request, the Treasurer shall exhibit the books and accounts of the Corporation to any officer or Council member of the Corporation. He or she shall perform all the duties incident to the office of Treasurer, subject at all times, however, to the control of the Council. The Treasurer shall, if required by the Council, give such security for the faithful performance of his or her duties as the Council may require.

ARTICLE V—CONTRACTS, CHECKS, AND BANK ACCOUNTS

Section 1: **Checks, Notes, and Contracts.** The Council is authorized to select such banks or depositories as it shall deem to be proper for holding the funds of the Corporation. The Council shall determine who shall be authorized to sign checks, drafts or other orders for the payment of moneys, to sign acceptances, notes or other evidences of indebtedness, to enter into contracts or to execute and deliver documents and instruments on the Corporation's behalf.

Section 2: **Investments.** The funds of the Corporation may be retained in whole or in part in cash or be invested and reinvested from time to time in such property, real, personal and otherwise, or in stocks, bonds or other securities, as the Council may consider desirable.

ARTICLE VI—OFFICE AND BOOKS

Section 1: **Office.** The office of the Corporation shall be located at such place as the Council may from time to time determine.

Section 2: **Books.** There shall be kept at the office of the Corporation, or such other place as the Council shall designate, correct books of account of the activities and transactions of the Corporation, including a minutes book, which shall contain a copy of the Certificate of Incorporation, a copy of these by-laws, and all minutes of the meetings of the Council.

ARTICLE VII—FISCAL YEAR

The fiscal year of the Corporation shall be determined by the Council.

ARTICLE VIII—INDEMNIFICATION

The Corporation shall indemnify its Council members and officers in the manner and to the full extent provided by the Not-for Profit Corporation Law of the State of New York, and, except as prohibited in that law, the Corporation may provide additional indemnification pursuant to agreement, action of the Council, or provision of these by-laws.

ARTICLE IX—AMENDMENT OF BY-LAWS

These by-laws may be amended at any meeting of the Council by consensus of the Council members present at the meeting.

Appendix B

Day - To - Day

In this appendix you will find a variety of lists, letters, forms and surveys that reflect TALC's growth and development throughout the years. My added comments are in italics.

Questionnaires

From time to time questionnaires are sent to parents and children to determine how things are going, get ideas for new directions and offerings, and keep lines of communication open.

On the next few pages are questionnaires that were broadly distributed at the end of TALC's first year of operation, when financial considerations, uneven parent participation, and a possible move were factors. At the time these questionnaires were developed, TALC did not specify family involvement and work requirements.

The Alternative Learning Center
Questions

Please circle yes or no, fill in appropriate blanks and feel free to add pertinent information in the margins.

1. Would your family like to make use of The Alternative Learning Center in the Fall 92 / Spring 93 year?

     YES   NO

     If so, please list the ages of any children you would bring to the Center.

     AGES: _____, _____, _____, _____

2. Do the hours of 1:00 to 3:00 on Tuesday and Thursday generally work for your family?

     YES   NO

3. Would you like to see the Center open:

On Saturdays?	YES	NO
After school?	YES	NO
Mornings?	YES	NO
During the summer?	YES	NO

4. Would you come for drop-in days occasionally (when no workshops are scheduled)?

YES   NO

5. Would you be willing to become members at a cost of $50/half year; $100/full year per family?

YES   NO

If not, would a lower fee induce you to join?
YES   NO
If it would, how much would you pay?

$_____/half year $_____/full year

6. Would you be willing/able to pay a reasonable workshop fee over and above your membership fee?

YES   NO

PLEASE NOTE: Membership fees are used to pay rent and insurance for our meeting space and to cover publicity. The cost, if any, for the workshops themselves must be covered by the individual workshop fees.

continued on next page

7. Are you willing/able to lend your time, energy and/or organizational skills to help run the Center? We strongly encourage each family to lead one workshop (approx. 1 hour long) each semester. YES   NO

8. The following are some possible projected workshops for the Fall 92 / Spring 93 year. Please indicate any your child(ren) would be interested in attending, including the number and ages of children. (NOTE: No commitment is implied. We are only trying to determine interest.)

WORKSHOP   Y/N   # KIDS   AGES
Theater and dance   _____ _____ _____
Bookbinding   _____ _____ _____
Science Experiments_____ _____ _____
(The list continued with fifteen more suggestions.)
Suggestions for other workshops:

9. The following field trips are being considered for the Fall 92 / Spring 93 year. Please indicate those that interest you. (Again, no commitment is intended.)

FIELD TRIP   Y/N
Glass Blowing   _____
Hospital Tour   _____
(More were listed.)
Suggestions for other field trips:

Please take a moment to comment on The Alternative Learning Center's first year, keeping in mind that any observations, positive and negative, will help us direct the Center's growth.
Compliments:

Complaints:

Suggestions:

Thank you for your time in answering these questions. Your input will be used to make three basic decisions about the future of The Alternative Learning Center.

1. Whether The Alternative Learning Center should continue at all.
2. If so, in what format.
3. Whether we can afford the luxury of a site such as the Morris Memorial.

If you return this questionnaire, we'll keep you posted!
Name
Address   Phone
_____ Check here if you want to be notified of the time and place of the next Alternative Learning Center Meeting.
Please return this questionnaire by Friday, July 3, 1992 to:
(*Member's name and address given here.*)

The following Adult Interest Survey and Youth Interest Survey were used when the planning process was more informal, before the Workshop Proposal Form was developed.

The Alternative Learning Center, Inc.
Chatham, New York
Adult Interest Survey

TALC is interested in knowing what you, the parent/guardian, would most like the center to provide for your child(ren). Please take a few minutes to complete these forms and return them to (member's name) before May 18th. The address is listed at the end of each form. TALC plans to use this information to assist in planning workshops and field trips in the future. There will be no follow-up phone call, so please return the forms as soon as you can. Thank you for your time and interest.

A. What particular skills or interest areas would you like to have TALC offer for your child?
1.
2.
3.

B. Would you join and/or participate in the Center if the above skills or interest areas were offered?
_____ yes   _____ no

C. How will class size, day of week, time of day, or age of participants affect whether your child(ren) will participate in a given activity?

D. What types of field trips would you and your child(ren) enjoy with the Center?
1.
2.
3.

E. Is there a hobby, skill or interest that you might be willing to teach / share with a group of children? If so, please specify.

Description:
Age group: _____   Number of participants: _____
Space and materials needed:
Number of assistants, if needed: _____

F. If you know anyone who would be willing to share an interest or teach a specific workshop, please list their name(s), address(es) and phone number(s) below.

Return before May 18 to (*member's address here*)

The Alternative Learning Center, Inc.
Chatham, New York
Youth Interest Survey

TALC wants to find out more about what YOU are interested in learning and doing. Please fill out this form the best you can by yourself or with an adult. Be as specific as you can so TALC can follow your interests in planning future workshops and field trips.

Name
Address
Phone   Age

A. What do you like to spend your time doing? (Hobbies and/or interests)

B. If you like to collect things, what are they?

C. Of all the things that you own, what do you like the most?

D. What kind of field trips would you enjoy?

E. What kinds of activities using things or objects would you like to do with other kids? (example - Legos)

F. What games would you enjoy doing with other people? (example - board games)

G. What creative activities would you like to do with other people? (example - music)

H. What activities in Science would you like to do? (example - experiments)

I. What particular skill(s) would you like to learn more about? (example - computer)

Continued on next page

J. What particular people/culture/time would you be interested in learning more about?

K. Is there anything else you would like to learn how to do (skill) or enjoy doing with others? (Mixed age groups or your own age)

L. If you would be willing to teach a skill or share an interest, please let us know what it is.

M. Please let us know what your favorite workshop(s) and/or field trip(s) with TALC have been.

Return form to (*member's address here*)

Workshop/Field Trip Proposal Sheets

On the next page is an example of the proposal sheet that each family currently fills out before each session to meet its obligation to provide an activity for the upcoming session. The Morris Memorial is the name of the community building which is TALC's current home (and was also its home during the first year).

The Alternative Learning Center
Chatham, New York
Workshop/Field trip Form

Class or Activity Title:
Description:

Materials to bring:

Ages: Date & Time:

Rain date or other possible dates & times this activity can be offered:

Instructor's Fee: Materials Fee:

Enrollment Information

Minimum: Maximum:

Coordinator:
Name:

Address:

Phone:

Instructor's Name & Phone (if different from coordinator):

Location of Activity
_____ Morris Memorial   _____ Other (please specify)

Directions: (please use reverse side)
Please get this form to the appropriate age group coordinators before the planning meeting. (*Names & phone numbers are listed here - the three divisions include: 5 and under, Ages 6-9, and Ages 10+.*)

Officers and Jobs

The following lists were drawn up in TALC's "middle" years to detail some of the ongoing positions and jobs involved in running the learning center. Many of the jobs which previously were done by one, two or three people are now more widely shared or done by committee.

Some have evolved; for example, the responsibility for maintaining class lists and fielding questions about particular classes has been distributed to the individuals who have arranged for the events / classes. There is also currently a Registrar, and a volunteer who handles TALC trips to performances and the theater.

These lists are from a brochure that describes specific offices and positions held by people at TALC. Also included are descriptions of the Parent Assistant and Clean-Up duties, which have evolved over time. In these documents, my comments are in italics.

How TALC Works

We are a group of children and parents interested in creating a relaxed, enjoyable learning environment where we can share skills and interests. Parents teach many of the workshops, assist at all of the workshops, and oversee a play area which is provided for siblings who are not participating in the schedules workshop. TALC is guided by a Council, consisting of any interested members and the following officers and volunteers.

TALC Officers

Coordinator(s) - Responsible for planning the calendar for each learning session, including contacting facilitators and booking field trips; scheduling and coordinating meetings; arranging a facility / space; preparing the brochure for each session; handling registrations and preparing / maintaining class lists for each activity.

Treasurer - Responsible for maintaining the checking account; a general ledger; and accounts receivable (tuition fees, membership fees) and accounts payable (rent, instructors' fees, insurance, and other bills).

Secretary - Responsible for maintaining the database of the mailing list (including members' lists, taking names and address); taking minutes at meetings and making those available to officers and members; and sending notices of meetings.

Member at Large - Responsible for coordinating other volunteer positions (listed below); serving as general contact with membership; assisting coordinator(s) as required.

Other Volunteer Positions

Parent Assistant Coordinator - Responsible for keeping track of the key(s) to TALC facilities; assigning parent assistants for each workshop activity; assuring that parent assistants are trained.

Parent Agreement Coordinator - Responsible for explaining parent agreement and youth contract; mediating any problems; serving as liaison to the Council.

Children's Activities for Meetings - Responsible for facilitating children's activities for Opening Day, the planning meeting, and the evaluation / annual meeting.

Data Entry Support - Responsible for designing / formatting brochure and producing camera-ready copy.

Parent Assistant

At one time, each family was called upon to provide a parent assistant for the workshop the family was attending. The following document was given to families in their registration packets on Opening Day, along with the date(s) when someone from that family would be responsible to act as parent assistant. Care was taken to assign people to workshops for which they had registered. This document is from the days when TALC met at the church.

Parent Assistant Information

We need you to be the Parent Assistant at the following workshop(s): _____

_____

Please mark your calendar with this workshop. If you are unable to serve as the Parent Assistant for this workshop, please notify _____ ASAP!

If this is a series, the other Parent Assistants are:

_____

_____

Duties of a Parent Assistant

1. Pick up keys.

2. Arrive at least half an hour before the workshop starting time.

3. Unlock doors.

4. Turn on lights and turn up heat.

5. Unlock supply room door. Take toys, bulletin board, and "drop" box out of the closet.

6. Greet instructor and help him/her set up.

7. Check-in children on the class list and record any designated adults as necessary. Notify _____ or _____ if a child is left at the workshop without a parent or other designated adult.

8. Assist during workshop.

9. Oversee general clean-up – put toys, etc. back in the supply closet; replace any rearranged furniture; sweep floor.

10. Turn down the thermostat and turn off lights.

11. Return keys.

Clean-up

In the early years of the center, clean-up was informal and fairly simple. Now that many more families are involved, different strategies for clean-up have been employed.

From a 9/98 letter to members:

"A new clean-up crew team idea has been created for this semester for children over age 8. All children ages 8 and up have been assigned to three clean-up duty assignments and children age 7 have been assigned to one as an introduction. Where possible clean-up assignments have been made on days when it appears your child will be attending the last class of the day. If you cannot attend on your clean-up day it is your responsibility to find a replacement for yourself. All parents are responsible for ensuring that their child's task is completed properly. In the mailbox there is a clipboard with clean-up assignments listed for check-off by your child."

Appendix C

Smorgasbord:

TALC's Offerings

Here we have a sampling of classes and activities offered at TALC over the years. Some, such as creative movement, theater arts, foreign languages, science experiments, certain crafts (knitting, sewing, woodworking), chorus, open stage, holiday events, etc. are repeated from year to year.

Two major events that happen each year are the Display Day at the end of each session and the annual TALC Picnic in the spring. This list is offered to inspire you and spark your creativity as you consider your local resources and needs.

Quilting

Puppetry and the Art of Story Creation

Creative Movement

Theater Workshop

American Sign Language

Woodshop

Microscope Class

Nature Study

May Day Workshop Celebration

Herbal workshop

Pumpkin Carving

Walking with Wildlife

Drawing

Mud, Sand and Water

Monoprint

Stamp Printmaking

Felt-Making

Kitchen Sink Instruments

Basic Horse Care (Or Hints for the Horse-Happy)

People in Your Neighborhood - Series includes Police Force, Post Office, Flower Shop, Dentist's Office

Mural Story

Movement in Nature

Wood Sculpture

Games Day

Math I and Math II

Tumbling

Write and Illustrate Your Own Book

Wrapping Paper

Button Shirts (decorating a shirt with buttons)

Bread Baking

Science-By-Mail

Skating

Indoor Swimming

Gym & Games

President's Day Workshop

Knitting

American Indians - Today and Yesterday

Pysanky: Ukrainian Easter Eggs

Easter Crafts

Making Ethnically Diverse Waldorf Style Dolls

Cardboard Corner - making toys out of corrugated cardboard boxes

Painting

Chinese Flowers

Singing with Friends

Exploring a Fresh-water Lake

Gyroscope/Boomerang

Conversational French

Foundations of American Freedom

Colonial America

Pocket dolls

Toddler Time – dress-ups, songs, finger plays, tea party

Map Mania

Cooperative Games

Papier Mache Sculpture

Newsletter Production

Basic Aid Training

First Aid for Children Today

Make Your Own Rainstick

Beeswax Candle Dipping

Valentine's Day Crafts

Revolutionary America

Super Sandals – making sandals from a newspaper!

Kitchen Kapers – food projects

Paper Basket Weaving

Animal Tracking

Chick Incubation

The Magic of Music – music appreciation

A Trip to Senegal – slide show & display of native items

Designing Everyday Stuff

Wiggle Your Words: Exploring Poetry with Children

Nautical Knot-Tying

Japanese Ink Painting

Simple Structures/Basic Biology

Getting to Know Your Body

Globe Games – Geography

The "Unsinkable Titanic"

Explorers – Columbus and others (includes effect on indigenous peoples)

Scary Stories – writing workshop

Let's Tell a Story

Creating a Cooperative Learning Center

Where Does Your Food Go? Introduction to the digestive system

Architecture

What Do You Live In?

Building Your Own Home

Sciencing with Snails

Gymnastics

Worms Eat My Garbage

Games from World Cultures

The Sprout Man – Grow Delicious Salads!

Little-People's Collage-Making

Mind Over Matter – properties of matter

How Does a Flower Grow?

Percussion Discussion – with Mikie the Drum-head Fat Boy!

Cooking With Solar Energy

Introduction to Sailing

The Orchestra

Beginning Spanish

Aikido

Yoga

Playback Theater – improvisational & interactive

Mummies, Myths and Hieroglyphics

Sewing with Felt

Prehistoric Native Americans

Papermaking

African American History

Pioneer Homecrafts

Tropical Reef

Money Skills for Mini-Managers

Watercolor Painting

Reading Music for Beginners

Story Club

What Do I Do Now? Problem-solving

Clowning Around – juggling

Board Game Creating

Open Stage

Basic Elements of Art: Primary & Secondary Colors

Systems of the Body

Introduction to Horseback Riding

Let's Jumprope!

Chorus

Silk Ribbon Embroidery

Let's Eat Japan

Sculpey Workshop

Drumming

Gleaning

Dealing With Addition

Antarctica!

Beadie Babies – making beaded critters

Fingerprinting: its history and uses

Our Amazing Earth: Hands-On Geology

Hot Car Swap: Matchbox and Hotwheels Car Trade

A Brief History of Jazz

Introduction to Letters and Numbers

Paper Airplanes

Solar Car Construction

Waterways of New York

Yearbook

Fairy Tales

Field trips:

Columbia Memorial Hospital

Albany Institute of History and Art: Perceptions Games; The Artists' Craft; Adventures in Imagination

Channel 13 Television Station

A Visit to the Chiropractor!

Rensselaer County Junior Museum: Seeing the Seasons

Miss Bee Haven Apiary

To Climb a Waterfall

Old Chatham Sheepherding Company

Albany Planetarium

Winter Sky – Astronomy

Tour of the Times-Union newspaper operation

New York State Capitol

Freihofer's Bakery

Spelunking Trip

Olana Historic Site Museum

Reptile Man

Clermont State Historic Site

Threshold Seed Company – biodynamic seed company

Teddy Bear Picnic

Shaker Heritage Society

Norman Rockwell Museum

Jonas Studio Tour – wildlife and dinosaurs

Zoe's Pet Extravaganza – pet show!

Ko-Motion – mime, clowning, dance & drama

Berkshire Museum

Rocketry and Space Flight Program, Aerosciences Museum

Young Person's Ballet Series

Darrow School Environmental Center

Sail on the Clearwater

Junk Music with the Junk Man

New York State Museum

Howe Caverns

Sheep and Wool

Erie Canal Lock Tour

Camping Trip

Trip to the Chatham Firehouse

Trip to the Veterinarian

Gumear Dairy Farm

Tipple Lumber Mill

Plays at The "Egg" – theater in Albany

Mad Hatter Tea Party

Homemade Pizza Party

Holiday Songs and Stories with Bill Cliff

Hancock Shaker Museum

Wilde Fire Company – Custom-built fire engines!

Face to Face: An Introduction to Portraits

Living History in the Victorian Era: Brown House Inn, Amsterdam

Appendix D

Things To Consider

Working with The Alternative Learning Center and talking with people about their efforts in different parts of the country inspired me to offer some meetings for people interested in starting such centers. Some of the handouts from those workshops are included in this Appendix. If you wish to have a workshop in your area, contact me at 518-392-6900.

Starting a Parent Cooperative School / Learning Center
Things to Consider

Is there a need? Finding others in your area who are interested; conducting a needs/interest survey; assessing if there are sufficient interest and people who will be committed to making it work.

What is your philosophy / purpose?

Will the program be a full-time school or part-time supplemental program (for public, private, or homeschooling families)? Are program offerings for children only, or will there be adult classes as well?

Should your program be affiliated with an existing school or program which is in accord with your philosophy / purposes?

What are the requirements in your state for private schools, home education programs, etc. What about incorporation, chartering, accreditation, tax-exempt status, etc.? Do you know a lawyer who can help you with this work?

How will the program be structured, and how will decisions be made? Consensus or majority vote or a combination? With a council or steering committee or board of directors? With a director who is either "in charge" or who acts as liaison between the council or board and the program?

What kind of insurance will the program require?

What kind of facility will be needed, if any?

How will the program be funded? Possibilities include: fees for services (tuition or membership, set fee or per session fee), grants, fund-raising events, government money (charter schools, vouchers).

What kind of services will be offered? Will children be divided into groups / classes? If so, how? Will the program accommodate children with special needs?

Will teachers / workshop leaders be hired, or will the program rely on parents and other volunteers (or a combination)?

How will parent participation be structured? Should there be a work requirement of X amount of hours a month, or X number of workshops presented per semester? What kinds of work will fulfill the requirements – inside and outside the "classroom"? Will child care be available for younger children of participating parents? What happens to parents who do not meet the work requirements?

Can families be asked to leave the program? For what reasons? Will there be a means of appeal?

How will the program be advertised?

Insurance

The question of insurance invariably arises early in discussions about starting alternative schools or learning centers. The following is a non-exhaustive list of various types of insurance which are available for these types of programs. Not all of these types of coverage are needed by all programs, and many groups start with only General Liability Insurance.

• **General Liability Insurance** – Insurance against personal injury or property damage. The insurer will pay claims established by a lawsuit and may settle some claims without the need for a lawsuit. It does not generally cover accidents to students in schools. This is probably the most common form of insurance for school/learning center type programs.

• **Accident insurance** – Covers injury to students.

• **Employment Insurance** – Includes Workers' Compensation, Disability Benefits, and Unemployment Insurance. For programs which have employees. Requirements vary from state to state.

• **Automobile Insurance** – Required for vehicles owned in the name of the organization. Also available for non-owned automobiles for a fairly small charge. General Liability Insurance policies may exclude auto accidents.

• **Property Insurance** – Covers organization's personal property, such as equipment.

• **Directors and Officers Insurance** – Covers wrongful acts or decisions of directors and officers of the organization. For example, claims such as discrimination.

It is advisable to discuss the needs of your particular program with an insurance agent to determine which types of insurance are necessary, desirable, and/or affordable.

Appendix E

Sample Registration Form

   The document on the following pages is an actual registration form used by The Alternative Learning Center in Spring 1999. On the actual form, after each course offering a coordinator is listed; to protect privacy I have not included those names and phone numbers on this sample form. These forms are sent out before a semester begins and are returned before Opening Day, with half the total payment,.

The Alternative Learning Center
Spring 1999

The Alternative Learning Center is proud to be continuing its eighth year. We are a cooperative endeavor organized and run by member parents. Parents teach many of our workshops, assist at all of the activities and clean up, and oversee a play area which is provided for siblings who are not participating in the scheduled workshop. (PLEASE NOTE: WE ARE NOT A DROP-OFF CENTER, REGARDLESS OF THE AGE OF YOUR CHILDREN). If circumstances arise and you are unable to attend a session with your child(ren), please arrange with another adult member to be responsible for your child in your absence.

Registration

Membership is required for all activities (visitors are welcome). Membership costs $35 per family per semester. There is a $16 per child insurance surcharge (paid once annually, normally in September, unless you are new members registering mid-year) that we are obligated to collect to assure that we have proper insurance coverage.

Pre-registration is required for all workshops and field trips, even those which are free of charge. We strongly urge you to send your registration by Friday, January 15.

REGISTER EARLY! Enrollment is limited. Aside from written confirmation handed out on Opening Day (January 20, see schedule), you will only be notified if a workshop you have chosen has been closed out.

FEES AND PAYMENT: A 50% deposit for the membership fee and combined courses is due with this registration form. Please be prepared to pay the remaining 50% on Opening Day as we are unable to hold your place in classes if payment is not received. Most courses are free to members, unless otherwise noted. Please pay close attention to your choices. Except for extreme cases or in the case of class cancellation, class fees and registration are non-refundable.

Each workshop is being coordinated by a member; if you have any questions about a specific activity, please call that workshop coordinator. Please also do call the coordinator listed if you can't attend a workshop, to allow someone on the waiting list to take your place.

The age ranges given for the workshops are guidelines. You are the best judge of your child's abilities; however, please ask before including an older or younger child.

LOCATION: Unless otherwise indicated, workshops are held at the Morris Memorial, Park Row, Chatham, NY. There is limited on-street parking on Park Row or you may park at the beginning of the block in the old train station parking lot. For information or if you have any general questions please call ___ or ___, our Coordinators. We look forward to your joining us!

Meetings

The input of particpating families is vital to The Alternative Learning Center.

COUNCIL MEETINGS – At these meetings, we will review our finances, address any issues which have come up, and attend to administrative details. Anyone who is interested in participating is welcome and will have an equal vote! Children are welcome for quiet play during the meetings, if they do not have other scheduled activities.

COUNCIL MEETINGS
Dates:
Mon. 2/1. 11-12 noon
Wed. 2/24. 10-11 am
Wed. 3/3, 10-11 am

LONG TERM PLANNING MEETING – At this meeting we will discuss the future direction of TALC - do we hire an administrator or divide coordinator duties into several positions to be handled by members...if you have strong feelings on this, please attend this meeting, as a vote will be taken. And, please, nursing babies only at this meeting. Thursday, February 4, 6:30 pm.

FALL SEMESTER PLANNING MEETING – At this evening meeting, we will firm up our selections for the FALL session. Remember that all families are requested to volunteer to teach or coordinate at least four hours of workshop, activity or field trip time. Older children who wish to participate in the meeting are welcome. Wednesday, 4/7, 6:30-8:30 pm.

DISPLAY DAY! Wednesday, April 28th, 10 am to noon. Display Day offers our participants an opportunity to share the results of various activities that they have undertaken throughout the session. In addition to projects completed in Learning Center Workshops, children and youth are invited to bring in other home education projects for our Display Day. Don't miss it!!!

Workshops

1.   (01Open) Opening Day – Everyone participating in the Spring session is expected to attend for registration confirmation, to meet other member families, and to learn about the Learning Center's space, policies, and division of responsibilities. This includes both veteran members and new participants. Final payment will be due at this time. Children's activities will be provided...you've all heard of "track and field"... well, welcome to "TALC and Field"...call B. if you want to help. DATE: Wednesday, 1/20, 10 - 12 noon

2.   (02ADD) Dealing With Addition – Using a deck of cards, we will explore basic number combinations and simple math problems. Suitable for beginning math students.
Materials to bring: Deck of cards
Ages: 5 - 7
Date & Time: Wed. 3/24, 11 - 12 noon
Min. 5 / Max. 10

3.   (03ANT) Antarctica! Learn about this fascinating region: its exploration, wildlife, and current scientific research. Participants should have access to a computer and the internet.
Ages: 7 - 9
Date & Time: Weds., 2/24. 3/3. 11 - 12 noon
Min. 5 / Max. 12

4.   (04BEABAB) Beadie Babies – Come and learn how to make your choice of two very cute Beadie Babies - the gecko or the snake. Beadie Babies are small easy-to-make beaded critters that range from three to seven inches in size. This is a child-led workshop.
Materials to bring: scissors
Fee: $1 per person
Ages: 7+ (younger OK but parent must stay)
Date & Time: Mon., 1/25, noon - 1 pm

5.   (05CHOR) Chorus – The instructor, S.B.M., will lead children in vocal warm-ups, songs and games, with Session III concentrating on more complicated rhythms, exercises and songs. Older children in II may also take III. The age ranges listed are flexible; please feel free to check with the class coordinator if you have any questions. Eight classes. Classes are not listed individually on your calendar. Please consult this schedule for exact times.
Session I - Ages 4 - 6 (45 minutes); Session II - Ages 6 - 10 (45 minutes); Session III - Ages 10 - 14 (30 minutes)

Instructor Fees: Sessions I or II - $20@, Session III - $12@, combined taking of Sessions II and III - $32@

Min. 10 / max. 15

Dates & Times: Weds., 2/24, 3/3, 3/10, 3/17, 3/24, 3/31, 4/7, 4/14

Session I - 10 - 10:45; Session II - 10:45 - 11:30;Session III - 11:30 - 12 noon

6. (06CREAT) Creative Movement with K.D. – This will be an opportunity to discover new ways of moving and increasing our range of motion. Using stories and theater games,we will work on a dramatization based on children's literature. The last session will be an "open class" for parents, siblings, and other interested Learning Center members. Instructor: K.D.

Ages: 4 - 7

Fee: $21 for six classes

Date & Time: Weds., 1 - 2 pm; 2/24, 3/3, 3/10, 3/17, 3/24, 3/31

7. (07FINGPR) Fingerprinting – Learn about history and value of fingerprints. We will also learn to do fingerprinting. Instructor: R.N.

Min. 4 / max. 12

Ages: 10 and up

Date & Time: Mon., 3/1, 11 - 12 noon

8. (08FRENCH) French Club – Parlez-vous Francais? Un peu? Tres bien! If you already have a bit of French vocabulary, come join us for a half-hour of conversation practice. Each week I will pass out a new sheet of vocabulary and conversation on one topic (e.g. breakfast, lunch, dinner, sports, vacation, home life, etc.) and the next week we will try to converse on the topic, incorporating phrases and vocabulary from previous weeks. This class is strictly practice, all learning will be done at home before classes.

Ages: all with a definite interest; all participants should already know numbers to 100, colors, and basic greeting phrases. Parents, please attend.
Min./max. - none
Date & Time - Weds., 12:30 - 1 pm; 1/27, 2/3, 2/24/ 3/3, 3/10, 3/17, 3/24, 3/31, 4/7, 4/14

9.   (09GEOG) Geography – Starting close to home, we will pull together what we already know about the physical world around us and how it affects our lives. We will gradually widen our focus to include the surrounding region. Note: we may have field trips and other get-togethers interspersed between the five scheduled classes.
Ages: 9+ (no younger, please). Min.1 / max. 10
Date & Time: Mon. 1 - 2 pm; 3/15, 3/22, 3/29, 4/5, 4/12

10.   (10GEOL) Our Amazing Earth! Hands-on Geology – In this 4-session geology workshop, kids will take a look at our active earth, the forces that shape it, and resources within it. Projects and activities related to weekly topics will be part of each session.
A field trip to the New York State Museum for a geology program is planned in conjunction with the workshop.
Materials to Bring: TBA
Date & Time: Mon. 10 am; 3/8, 3/15, 3/22, 3/29
Ages: 6 - 9 (presentations will be geared to 6 - 9 year olds, but older students are welcomed to join - for learning and to help with projects).
Min.6 / max.12

11.   (11HANDWK-1) Handwork #1 – This class will teach the felting of wool and basic stitching projects. Instructor: C.O.
Ages: 6 - 8. Min.3 / max.8
Fee: $32 for six 1-hour workshops
Dates & Times: Mon., 12 - 1 pm; 3/1, 3/15, 3/22, 3/29, 4/5, 4/12

12.   (12HANDWK-2) Handwork #2 –
We will dye yarn with natural plants and use it to make a handwork project, possibly a crochet animal puppet. Instructor: C.O.
Ages: 9+. Min.4 / max.8
Fee: $30 for five 1-hour workshops
Dates & Times: First class to be held at C.'s house; all others will be at TALC. C.'s house on Fri., 2/26, 1 pm. At TALC: Mon., 1 - 2 pm, 3/1, 3/15, 3/22, 3/29

13.   (13HOME) Homeschool 101 –
Come share your ideas and concerns, resources and struggles with other home educating parents. Some sessions will have a specific focus, such as quarterly reports, or a guest speaker; most will be open to your needs. Parents and nursing infants only, please (other children will have gym time available).
Ages: parents
Date & Time: Wed., 1 - 2 pm; 1/27, 2/3, 2/24, 3/3, 3/10, 3/17, 3/24, 3/31 4/7, 4/14

14.   (14HORSE) Care and Riding of Horses –
This is a thorough introduction to horses, the equipment needed and its purpose, basic vaulting techniques, bareback riding and so much more. If you would like to really understand horses, this is the class to take. Instructor: C.S., B.R. Stables.
Ages: 4+
Materials needed: sturdy shoes or boots (parents too!) and helmets
Date & Time: Six Tuesday mornings; 4/6, 4/13, 4/20, 4/27, 5/4, 5/11
90 minutes each, exact times TBA
Fee: $45 per child. Min.12 / max. 24

15.   (15HOTCAR) Hot Car Swap: Matchbox and Hotwheels car trade – Bring your old and not-so-favorite-but-in-good-condition Hotwheels or Matchboxes for trading and swapping.
Ages: 5+. Date & Time: Mon. 4/5, 11 am
Materials: cars to trade. Min. / Max.: none

16.	(16JAZZ) A Brief History of Jazz – Four 1-hour sessions following the history of jazz from Louis Armstrong through Swing and the BeBop Revolution to Avant Garde. We will listen to famous musicians' best recordings and discuss the changes they have made. Participants will hear the greatest jazz musicians in American history. Instructor: D.M.
Ages: 10+
Dates & Times: Weds., 3/3, 3/10, 3/17, 3/24; 10 11 am
Min.4 / max. none

17.	(17JRGYM) Junior Gym – Warm up with calisthenics, followed by organized relays and games for fitness and fun,
Materials: sneakers with non-marking soles
Ages 5 - 7
Dates & Times: Weds., 10 am; 1/27, 2/3, 2/24, 3/3

18.	(18KNIT) Knitting – Knit a square for a TALC afghan. Find us sitting with a basket of wool and knitting needles. Sit yourself down and knit a square. In the end, we'll put them together and give it to someone who is cold. Both beginners & experienced welcomed – children & adults usually above 7.
Ages: 7+
Time & Date: when we can

19.	(19KNOTS) Simple knots – We will learn and investigate a few useful knots.
Ages: 6 - 8. Min.2 / max. 12
Date & Time: Mon. 10 - 11 am, 1/25 & 2/1

20.	(20LETNUMB) Introduction to Letters and Numbers – We will hear a story pertaining to the letter we will study. We will draw a picture with block crayons and draw the letter. We will do movement, walking the form.
Ages: 5 - 7. Min.3 / max.8
Date & Time: Mon., 9:15 - 10 am; 1/25, 2/1, 2/8, 2/22

21.   (21OPSTG) Open Stage; – All are welcome to participate in this relaxed and fun event. Come and bring something to the group (or, if your prefer, just fill in the audience). Almost anything goes(!). Perform on a musical instrument, read a poem or story, tell a joke, show something you have made, bring slides from a trip, introduce us to a pet, sing a song, bring in something that interests you to show and tell about, do a jig...
Ages: all
Date & Time: Mon. 12 - 2 pm, 3/8 & 4/5

22.   (22PAPAIR) Paper Airplanes - Part II – To all those pilots out there, come take off for another high-flying paper airplane class! Instructors: T., E., and C., a student-led activity.
Ages: 6+
Date & Time: Mon. 2/8, 12 noon - 1 pm
Min.0 / max.12

23.   (23POINDA) Pioneer Days – Come explore some of the activities common to American pioneer / Native American families through music, crafts, making butter by hand, Native American circle dances and games, pioneer songs and square dances and more. M. and M. are working on a list of stories and resource materials. If anyone is interested in reviewing them before the class, call.
Materials to Bring: any supplies needed will be discussed at the first class.
Ages: 4 - 6
Date & Time: Mon. 10 - 11 am, 1/25, 2/1, 2/8, 2/22, 3/1
Min.5 / max. 10

24.   (24ROCKS) Take Another Look at Rocks – The rocks all around us are used in many ways. In this two session workshop kids will "play" with rocks to learn about some common uses - such as in jewelry and for building and art materials.
Materials to bring: details to follow
 Ages: 4 - 6
Date & Time: Mon. 11 am, 3/15, 3/22
Min.4 / max.8

25.   (25SCI) Science Is – We will continue to explore the fascination and fun of science through experiments, projects, games and puzzles. This is a continuation of the fall science class. Enrollment is limited to children who participated in the fall, plus there is room for two additional newcomers.
Ages: 6 - 9
Dates & Times: Mon. 10 am, 1/25, 2/1, 2/8, 2/22, 3/1
Min.2 / max.8

26.   (26SOLAR) Solar Car Construction – Build a solar car while learning the mechanics and scientific theory needed to design a car. This is an eight-week program in which participants will work in teams of 2 - 3 and follow through on all stages of designing and building a solar car. The Departments of Energy, Conservation, and Education have developed this program as an innovative way to teach science, design skills, problem solving and the opportunity to work in a group. They also sponsor state and regional races in which we can participate if we choose. Geared for Middle School level – we will be including ages 9 years old and up for children who have the interest and stick-to-it-iveness to construct a solar car.
Materials to bring: to be determined as workshops progress
Fee: $16, a charge for solar panels and engines
Ages: 9+
Date & Time: Mon., 10 - 11 am; 3/1, 3/8, 3/15, 3/22, 3/29, 4/5, 4/12, 4/26
Min.6 / max.15

27.   (27SPAN) Let's Speak Spanish II – A continuation of our ongoing Spanish class to include light conversation, games, projects and stories. This class is open to students who were previously enrolled in Spanish in the fall semester so that continuity and progression can be assured.
Ages: 5 - 7
Date & Time: Wed., 11:30 on 1/27, 2/24, 3/3, 3/10, 4/7, 4/14; 12 noon on 2/3
Min. / max. : limited to previously enrolled students with 2 semesters of Spanish - this is a progressive class.

28.   (28VAL) Valentine's Day Crafts – Come join us for fun holiday crafts.
Materials: smiles
Ages: all
Date & Time: Feb. 10, 10 - noon

29.   (29WATR) Waterways of New York – Have you ever thought about how many great rivers and major lakes there are in New York State? These waterways have had a profound effect on the history and development of our state. We will read about the history of the New York waterways, read and draw maps of the state, and learn about the explorers, colonists and military figures who discovered new ways to use these transportation resources. We will take a tour of the Erie Canal lock system (see field trips) and, weather permitting, we will schedule an extra visit to West Point and a hike on the Erie Canal.
Ages: 8+
Date & Time: Wed., 10 - 11 am; 4/7, 4/14
Min.4 / max.15

30.   (30YEAR) Yearbook – Let's start taking photos on Display Day and put together a yearbook for all the kids to remember TALC by. This class will teach older children a bit about photo composition and a lot about layout. Learn how to crop and size photographs, use the Pagemaker program and put together a publication with various sections. The goal will be to produce a yearbook for printing that gives each child at TALC a space for a photo or picture and a brief description of themselves, or to publish something they have written. We can also incorporate sections for artwork or creative writing if there is sufficient interest.
Ages: 8+
Date & Time: Mon. 10 - 11 am; 2/8. Mon. 11 - 12 noon; 3/15, 3/22. If there are scheduling conflicts, children may miss one or two classes.

---

31.   (31UNDFIV) Under Five Activities – If you have a child five or under, please join us for organized activities provided by parents from 9 - 11 am on Mondays and Wednesdays when TALC is in session. Some of our activities already scheduled include walking tours of nearby Chatham establishments, and ballet (taught by one of our older TALC students, L.B.M.). We will finalize a schedule for these two hours prior to Opening Day. All parents of involved children are expected to contribute to activities and supervision; however, involvement does not require that you attend TALC on both Mondays and Wednesdays. Please note that these activities overlap with some regular classes for 4 and 5 year olds and that supervised play time will still be provided for younger children during those classes. Outside of the 9 - 11 hours of organized activities, play space is still available for younger children registered in other classes. PLEASE NOTE: Because of space limitations on the calendar, I was unable to list Under Five activities on every Monday and Wednesday, but they do exist!
Date & Time: Mon. & Wed. 9 - 11am, ongoing

32.   (32NEWMEMB) New Member Meeting – This will be an informal meeting to get you familiar with TALC. We will touch upon your responsibilities as a TALC member, our bylaws, insurance policy, and help you organize a future class / field trip. There will be time for questions / answers. We only have an hour, please be on time - thanks. This is for both new members and recent members who wish to become more involved.
Date & Time: Wed. 10 - 11 am, 1/27

33.   (33FAIRY) Fairy Tales – Come enter the magical world of the Brothers Grimm. In each of the two classes, children will lose themselves in a few of Grimm's fanciful fairy tales. After each reading, children will create a storymap, showing how one event leads to another, with both drawings and explanations.
Dates & Times: Wed. 11 am, 3/3, 3/10
Min.2 / max.6

FIELD TRIPS

Activities occurring away from the Morris are listed as "field trips."

FT1 (FT1BAK) Beginning Baking – Learn basic ingredients and what they do, plus basic measuring. 1st week, muffins and quick breads; 2nd week, sourdough and yeast products; 3rd week, cake decorating. Classes to take place at my home.
Ages: 5 - 7
Dates & Time: Tues., 10 am, 2/9, 2/23, 3/2
Min.2 / max.6

FT2 (FT2CAP) Tour of Capitol Building in Albany – Join us for a guided tour of the Capitol in Albany.
Ages: 9+. Date & Time: end of April - TBA

FT3 (FT3CLEAR) Sail on the Clearwater – We are applying for the opportunity to sail on the Clearwater. The applications are reviewed after December 1st. The total cost is $850 for a three hour trip with an education program. The maximum group size is 50 and they require at least 50% of the group to be children. If we reach 50 people enrolled, the cost would be $17 per person. This course offering is being listed merely to see if we have the number of people needed to support this activity. Payment would come at a later date. Trip coordinator will be in touch.
Ages: 5+. Date & Time: TBA
Fee: $17 per person, to be collected after the application is accepted.
Max.50

FT4 (FT4DARROW) Darrow School Environmental Center – The Science Department will give us a tour of their new facility for breaking down waste water back to clean water...the first in the country!
Materials: dress for weather.. Ages: all
Date & Time: Thursday, April 22nd, time TBA

FT5 (FT5DOLLS) Making Ethnically Diverse Waldorf Style Dolls – Participants will choose one of six ethnically diverse dolls to make, clothe, and do a little background research on the part of the world you choose for your doll to come from. At the end of the classes (maybe at Open Stage?) we can present our dolls with a short talk/skit on where they come from. An option will be to design a simple ethnic outfit for them and we will attempt to make it. Minimal sewing skills appreciated - participants need to be prepared to work on dolls at home to complete each phase as necessary. Also, research should be done from home - I hope to have some great discussions about the world over our sewing! (Anyone with clothes-making experience would be welcome to give help and advice on the outfit-making!)
Materials: Sewing (cloth) scissors, and in later classes, material to make clothes. Or, you can buy an outfit if you prefer.
Ages: 10+ (younger if adult prepared to do most of the work)
Dates & Time: Thursdays, 9 - 11 am; 2/4, 2/11, 2/18, 2/25, 3/4, 3/11
Fee: $20 - this covers the cost of the doll kit and extra needles and thread that I will supply at the classes.
Min.5 / max.6

FT6 (FT6DANCE) Performances at The Egg - Dance Brazil – A vibrant and virtuosic company of dancers, singers and musicians. Dance Brazil brings to its audiences the rich, exciting culture of Brazil via a repertoire that ranges from traditional and contemporary Afro-Brazilian to modern dance. Under the direction of master capoeirista and acclaimed choreographer Jelon Vieira, the company is known for its "rich, explosive and intrepid dancing." Plan to stay after the performance for a backstage tour.
Ages: recommended ages 8+, but all welcome, each child (even babies) must have a ticket.
Date & Time: Friday, 3/26 at 10 am. Fee: $3.50 a ticket
Min.0 / Max.40 seats reserved.

FT7 (FT&JUNK) Junk Music with the Junkman – The Junkman uses over 120 pieces of junk, found objects and materials that have been discarded by others, to prove that anything can be used to make fun and exciting music and to learn a creative approach to recycling and reuse. Students are selected to join the Junkman in a junkjam.
Ages: geared to ages 10 - 14, but all welcome, everyone must have a ticket.
Date & Time: Weds. Feb. 3rd at 10 am
Fee: $3.50 a ticket
Min. / Max. 30 tickets ordered

FT8 (FT8LINC) Performance at The Egg – Steps of Lincoln – The year was 1939. Our nation was on the brink of another war to make the world safe for democracy. The world-renowned concert singer Marian Anderson was booked to play Constitution Hall. When the Daughters of the American Revolution learned that Ms. Anderson was black, the booking was cancelled. First Lady Eleanor Roosevelt refused to accept this bigotry and arranged for Ms. Anderson to sing on the steps of the Lincoln Memorial in a landmark public concert that helped mold the conscience of our nation.
Ages: geared to 8 - 15 years old
Date & Time: Mon. January 25, 10 am
Fee: $3.50 per ticket
Min. / Max. 30 tickets ordered

FT9 (FT9PETER) Performance at The Egg – Peter and the Wolf – Borrowing from the traditional Bunraku style of puppetry, Hudson Vagabond Puppets brings to life the classic children's story with their life-sized and larger-than-life-size creations and their cast of professional dancers and actors.
Ages: recommended ages 5 - 12 but all welcome
Date & Time: Friday, April 16, 10 am
Fee: $3.50 per ticket
Min. / Max. 40 tickets reserved

FT10 (FT10SCAR) Performance at The Egg – The Scarlet Letter – Written by Phyllis Nagy, this provocative and unusual adaptation of the Nathaniel Hawthorne American classic explores the impact of our nation's Puritan ethic on its people...past and present. Set in 17th century Boston, our resident theater company weaves this timeless tale with bold imagination and scintillating surprises that make this production chillingly contemporary. Special full-length production.
Ages: recommended for ages 13 - 18
Date & Time: Friday, March 19, 10 am
Fee: $3.50. Min. / Max. 20 tickets ordered.

FT11 (FT11GEOL) Field Trip to the New York State Museum for a Geology Program – A museum educator-led session on New York State geology. The focus will be on rocks and minerals of NYS and our mining and usage of them. This field trip is scheduled in conjunction with TALC workshop - Our Amazing Earth - Hands-On Geology.
Ages: 6+
Date & Time: tentatively set for March 23rd, time TBA. Min.10 / Max.25

FT12 (FT12HOWE) Field Trip to Howe Caverns and Iroquois Museum – Iroquois Museum will include tour of museum and workshop. They will have workshops for younger children and older children simultaneously. Then we will go a very short distance to Howe Caverns for a tour. Museum takes about one hour, caverns take about 1-1/2 hours. We should be finished about 12:30 pm, so you might want to bring a lunch and perhaps we can picnic together before returning home (weather permitting).
Ages: all
Date & Time: April 22, 9:30 am
Fee: fees for museum and cavern are complicated and depend on size of group and ages of people attending. My best estimate is $45 per family, which includes both activities and the workshop. Adjustments to fees will be made once sign-up for trip is complete.
Min.7 for group discount / Max.25

FT13 (FT13OLANA) Olana Tour and Activity – Tour of the painter Frederic Church's homestead (latter 19th century).
Date & Time: Thurs. April 29. 9 - 12 noon
Fee: $1 per person. Min. / Max. 40

FT14 (FT14PAINT) – Children's Painting Course – Painting classes include exercises such as experiencing single colors and their relationship to other colors, painting on colored background, creating simple motifs out of color relationships and relationship of color processes and nature processes. H. would like, especially for younger children, 1 adult helper per 4 children. Also appreciated would be help with clean-up. Helpers don't need to pay, of course. Instructor H.S., A. School of Painting.
SECTION I - Older Children, Ages: 8+
Date & Time: Monday at 3:30; 2/1, 2/8, 2/22, 3/1, 3/8, 3/15
Min.6 / Max.8
Fee: $48 for six weeks

SECTION II - Younger Children, Ages: 4 - 7
Date & Time: Wednesday at 2:30 pm; 2/3, 2/10, 2/24, 3/3, 3/10, 3/17
Min.4 / Max,7
Fee: $48 for six weeks

FT15 (FT15SHAK) Winter Weekend with the Shakers – Visit Hancock Shaker Museum and experience the Shaker way of life. See ice harvesting and go for a sleigh ride! Ages: all
Date & Time: Monday, Feb. 15 at 10 am
Fee: $9/adults; $2.50/students; pay at the door

FT16 (FT16SHEEP) Sheep and Wool – Introduction to the care of sheep and the preparation of wool. Participants will visit our farm during lambing season and will be shown basic aspects of care of the sheep. Participants will be given some wool from a sheep and will learn how to clean it and prepare it for spinning and other uses. Ages: all
Date & Time: TBA. Max.10

FT17 (FT17SPRING) 2nd Annual First Day of Spring Celebration – Join the S. for the first day of spring. Hide and picnic at Olana State Park. We are determined this year to prepare for any kind of weather (well, maybe excluding a blizzard) and definitely go for a brisk hike to greet the spring. Refreshments will be enjoyed at the park, if possible, or back at our home in Hudson. Dress appropriately and bring a snack to share.
Ages: all. Date & Time: Sat. March 20, 2 - 4 pm

FT18 (FT18BIKE) Wake Up Your Bike – Did you tuck your bicycle into bed this past autumn? (I didn't.) Let's get together and wake our bikes lovingly out of their slumber and show them how much we really do care for them. During session #1 (one hour) we will assess and begin minor repairs needed. Any work which should be completed by a professional will be indicated. (Please bring one or two adjustable crescent wrenches, pliers, Philips and regular screwdrivers, and a tire pump if you have one.) Session #2 (one hour) will be spent completing minor repairs as well as cleaning and lubricating our "machines." (Please bring bucket, rags, old toothbrushes, dish scrubbers, car wax, bicycle lubricant such as WD40.) We will be using a hose, so dress accordingly and expect the unexpected. Session #3 will be held at the Chatham Fairgrounds and we will participate in a "Bike Rodeo" (approximately two hours).
Ages: 8 and up. Min.0 / Max.10
Date & Time: Fri., 1 - 2 pm, 4/2 and 4/9; Fri., 1 - 3, 4/16
Location: Sessions 1 & 2 at S.; Session 3 at Chatham Fairgrounds

FT19 (FT19ERIE) Erie Canal Lock Tour – All families are invited to join the students in the Waterways of New York class for a tour of the Erie Canal Lock system. The tour is 90 minutes long and passes through two locks to demonstrate the operation of a canal and lock system. The tour will be provided by Crescent Cruises in Half Moon.
Ages: all. Min.20 / Max.76
Cost: $6 per person, ages 2 and under free
Date: Thursday May 13, 9:30 - 11:30 am

The Alternative Learning Center
Membership and Registration Form

Name:
Address:
Phone: Email address:
List names, ages, and birthdays of children:

Membership

_____ I understand that The Alternative Learning Center is a cooperative group and agree to contribute to programming as required and to assure that my children have a responsible adult in attendance at TALC with them.

_____ Please, do NOT include my name, address, phone number and children's birthdays on a list to be distributed to member families.

Workshop and Field Trip Registration

Wrkshp # Names of participants # of participants X Fee = Wrkshp total

Wrkshp #	Names of participants	# of participants X	Fee	Wrkshp total
01OPEN		____X	____	_____
02ADD		____X	____	_____
03ANT		____X	____	_____
04BEABAB		____X	_1.00_	_____
05CHOR: Sess. I		____X	20.00	_____
Sess. II		____X	20.00	_____
Sess. III		____X	12.00	_____
Sess. II/III		____X	32.00	_____
06CREAT		____X	21.00	_____
07FINGPR		____X	____	_____
08FRENCH		____X	____	_____
09GEOG		____X	____	_____
10GEOL		____X	____	_____
11HANDWK-1		____X	32.00	_____
12HANDWK-2		____X	30.00	_____
13HOME		____X	____	_____
14HORSE		____X	45.00	_____
15HOTCAR		____X	____	_____

174

Wrkshp #	Participants' names	# of participants	X	Fee	=	Wrkshp total
6JAZZ	_____	____	X	____		_____
17JRGYM	_____	____	X	____		_____
18KNIT	_____	____	X	____		_____
19KNOTS	_____	____	X	____		_____
20LETNUMB	_____	____	X	____		_____
21OPSTG	_____	____	X	____		_____
22PAPAIR	_____	____	X	____		_____
23PIONDA	_____	____	X	____		_____
24ROCKS	_____	____	X	____		_____
25SCI	_____	____	X	____		_____
26SOLAR	_____	____	X	16.00		_____
27SPAN	_____	____	X	____		_____
28VAL	_____	____	X	____		_____
29WATR	_____	____	X	____		_____
30YEAR	_____	____	X	____		_____
31UNDFIV	_____	____	X	____		_____
32NEWMEMB	_____	____	X	____		_____
33FAIRY	_____	____	X	____		_____

Subtotal for workshops #01 through #33 _____

Field Trips

Field trip #	Names of participants	# of participants	X	Fee	=	Trip total
FT1BAK	_____	____	X	____		_____
FT2CAP	_____	____	X	____		_____
FT3CLEAR	_____	____	X	later		_____
FT4DARROW	_____	____	X	____		_____
FT5DOLLS	_____	____	X	20.00		_____
FT6DANCE	_____	____	X	_3.50_		_____
FT7JUNK	_____	____	X	_3.50_		_____
FT8LINC	_____	____	X	_3.50_		_____
FT9PETER	_____	____	X	_3.50_		_____
FT10SCAR	_____	____	X	_3.50_		_____

Field trip # Names of participants # of participants X Fee = Trip total

Field trip #	Names of participants		# of participants	X Fee	= Trip total
FT11GEOL	_____		_____X _____		_____
FT12HOWE	_____		_____X 45.00		_____
FT13OLANA	_____		_____X _1.00_		_____
FT14PAINT	Sec.I	_____	_____X 48.00		_____
	Sec. II	_____	_____X 48.00		_____
FT15SHAK	_____		_____X _____		_____
FT16SHEEP	_____		_____X _____		_____
FT17SPRING	_____		_____X _____		_____
FT18BIKE	_____		_____X _____		_____
FT19ERIE	_____		_____X _6.00_		_____

Subtotal field trips _____

Subtotal for workshps _____

TOTAL FOR ALL ACTIVITIES _____

MEMBERSHIP (PER FAMILY / PER SEMESTER) $35 ___35.00__

Annual insurance surcharge per child (over 1 year old):

$16 x ___(# of children) = _____

TOTAL DUE _____

50% DEPOSIT ENCLOSED _____

Please make checks payable to The Alternative Learning Center.
Mail your deposit and the registration form to:
no later than Friday, January 8, 1999

Balance Due 1/20/99 _____(leave blank, please)

Appendix F

Other Learning Alternatives

    The Alternative Learning Center is not the only group learning option that was formed for homeschooling families in this geographical area. Two other learning alternatives which have provided programs for home educators are The Story Center *and* Lifelong Learning Through the Arts.

The Story Center

    The following is from a description of The Story Center, written by founder Ellen Broderick, and from a letter sent to parents before the beginning of the second year of operation of the center.

    The Story Center is a program designed to bring forth the natural fruition of the potentials that lie in each and every family and the children that compose it. It is called The Story Center for it is meant to enhance and encourage the natural expression and educated knowledge of the family, and to help the family develop, cherish, and add meaning to their own story as it unfolds each moment of each day of their lives. It is for individuals to recognize the interconnectedness of their own personal stories/learnings/dreams and how they come together to form the family and community stories/learnings/dreams which are essential to the quality of our lives. We are forming a place where learning is not in a vacuum, but is readily applicable to our lives and forms a foundation/building blocks for future interests, expressions and learning.

This program is for families who are homeschooling children between the ages of 6 and 12. It is offered four mornings per week from 8:30 to 1:00. On the fifth weekday, children are offered guidance in their pursuit of knowledge at a place of research (library, museum, etc.).

The Story Center assumes that children learn (w)holistically and that there is a crucial part played by parents and other family members in a child's education. As parents and teachers we look to support the child's natural wonder about reading, writing, speaking, science, mathematics, history and art. We model the importance of learning in the subjects in which learning is desired. We celebrate with children as they uncover the treasures innate in every subject. We begin with the interests and concerns of children and their families: Our teaching, then, celebrates what children know, and responds to what children do. Techniques that are learned during their writing workshop may well be used later to enhance their mathematics, social studies, or science curriculum. Likewise, something which has inspired a child in mathematics or social studies might become the topic of a writing project.

There are many opportunities for children to explore and become ever more proficient in social interactions. Children are encouraged to teach recently acquired information to peers. This has the double benefit of being a reinforcement of this knowledge for the child, and places the child in a leadership position. Individual and group dramatic presentations are an ongoing part of life at the center. The finest quality is the major criterion used while choosing play scripts and poetry to use for performances. Children are encouraged to share their own writing through dramatic presentation and/or public speaking. Each day opens and closes with a gathering of the full group, first to plan the day, and later to reflect upon it. Problem solving and gathering of knowledge is often a culmination of both group and individual efforts.

Each child will learn a healthy respect for the growing and development of his or her own body, and what it takes on a day to day basis to feed and nourish it. This will include the importance of attitude, hygiene, beauty, sun, fresh air, exercise, nature, pure water, warmth, rest, as well as proper food. These will be included so that they are seen as a part of a healthy lifestyle, and not done only when someone has lost their equipoise and is dysfunctional and/or sick.

The arts are seen as a vital part of our lives and are applied to all subjects. We also provide exposure to many art forms through in-house presenters who are fired up by what they do. A myriad of materials are available at The Story Center, and children are encouraged to explore these in a wide variety of ways.

The two main tools used to evaluate a child's progress are written evaluation (child's and teacher's) and portfolio. Children learn to keep records of their interests and progress. They review these with a teacher and parent, when possible, and plan future goals based on this review. It is our belief that children involved in this way are more invested in their education.

Our first year was filled with some of the most challenging and exciting learning, all of it educational, but not necessarily in the traditional sense of the word. Amen. We feel very blessed to have such a vision and such support for the foundation we have laid. We look forward to the new challenges and insights which the second year will bring. We invite you to become part of Our Story!

Lifelong Learning Through the Arts

The following is from a brochure about the program Lifelong Learning Through the Arts. From LLA founder Arnold Logan:

The necessity of educating our children evolves into self-development and self-education for the adults surrounding them: building community from inside out. A high quality of learning emerges when adult and child alike are involved in a process of development.

Created in 1996, Lifelong Learning Through the Arts is a Rudolf Steiner inspired, educational initiative. It reintroduces the concept of learning as an integral part of everyday family life in a non-institutional environment. A movement toward viewing one's life work as a lifelong unfolding process is the essence of a vision of work as art. The child is essentially an artist.

The Curriculum seeks to integrate the rigorous disciplines of literature, music, theater, movement and master crafts with the fundamental studies of arithmetic, reading, writing, foreign language, history, the natural and social sciences.

Our view is that the child is developmentally an artist, and may only lose artistic instincts later in life. LLA seeks to preserve the wonderment for learning, and prepares children for life. Students work within a group of mixed ages. Through partnerships in education we aim to expand the educational environment beyond the traditional institution.

Each morning the school community gathers together for singing, seasonal stories and announcements. Following this there is a two-hour main lesson in arithmetic, language arts, history or science. Before the lesson is presented and books are opened, the children are bathed in rhythmic movement of all sorts, poetry, song, recitation, and joy...

While LLA grew around the necessity of educating children, it has evolved into a center for supporting the development and education of both teachers and parents. Parents meet regularly to discuss issues as they arise in the educational process, and to share how to create learning environments in the home.

From LLA parent Ted Phelps: "This place looks like a home, and then again it looks like a school. This large 19th century country house does become quite school-like at 8:15 each Monday – Friday morning. The spirit of the home in the school and the school in the home, however, is, in fact, deeply intentional and is perfectly in synch with the idea that learning should take place in a familial environment."

Lifelong Learning Through the Arts is offered by Rose Harmony Association, Inc., 171 Water Street, Chatham, NY 12037; 518.392.7815; email <RoseHarmony@worldnet.att.com>

Resources

National organizations

Alliance for Parental Involvement in Education
PO Box 59
East Chatham, NY 12060-0059
518-392-6900
Fax: 518-392-6900
allpie@taconic.net

Alternative Education Resource Organization
417 Roslyn Road
Roslyn Heights, NY 11577
516-621-2195

Folk Education Association of America
Goddard College
123 Pitkin Road
Plainfield, VT 05667

National Coalition of Alternative Community Schools
1266 Rosewood, #1
Ann Arbor, MI 48104
734-668-9171

Charter School information:
Center for Education Reform
1001 Connecticut Ave. NW, Suite 204
Washington, DC 20036
800-521-2118

Publications

Growing Without Schooling Magazine
2380 Massachusetts Ave. Suite 104
Cambridge, MA 02140
617-864-3100

Home Education Magazine
PO Box 1083
Tonasket, WA 98855
800-236-3278

Journal of Family Life
22 Elm Street
Albany, NY 12202
518-471-9532

Paths of Learning: Options for Families and Communities
PO Box 328
Brandon, VT 05733-0328
www.great-ideas.org

Index

Costs. *See* Fees
Council 43, 119
Creativity 104, 107
Curriculum 54

D

Danford, Kenneth 96
Decision making 64, 121
Decker, Kate 50
Display Day 78
Diversity 53–58, 99
Documents 111. *See also* Bylaws

E

Educational reform 98

F

Families List 59
Family virtues 104
Fees 86. *See also* membership fees
Field trips 36, 168
Filanowska, Dorothy 40
Finances 83
Financial assistance. *See* TALCerships.
Funding xii

G

Gastil, John 96
General Liability Insurance 154

H

Home education 3–7, 67, 71, 73, 74, 91, 97, 105
Home Education Magazine 96
Home education requirements 76
Home instruction regulation 77
Home Schoolers' Exchange 7, 11, 10, 18
Homeschooling. *See* Home education.
Hornick, Joshua 96

I

Incorporation 30–31
Initial survey 19, 28
Insurance 30, 83, 84, 152, 153
Internet 88–90

J

Jennings, Kaylee 53, 57, 91
Judicial process 65

K

Kids Place of Choice 101
Koeser, Linda 95

L

Lawton, Beth 53, 60, 63, 72, 76, 77, 83, 86, 92
Leadership skills 100
Learning alternatives 78, 177
Learning centers xi, 74, 98
Learning Unlimited Network of Oregon (LUNO) 96
Lehman, Gene 89, 96
Lifelong Learning Through the Arts 78, 181
Logan, Arnold 181
LUNO. *See also* Learning Unlimited Network
Lyden, Linda 70

Ordering Information

To order *Creating a Cooperative Learning Center: An Idea-Book for Homeschooling Families*

• send $16.95 for each copy, plus
• $2.50 for shipping and handling of the first copy and $1.00 for shipping and handling of each additional copy,
• and in New York State the sales tax applicable to your county. (Under New York State law, sales tax must be calculated on the price of the book plus shipping and handling charges.)

• Foreign orders: please send US funds and include an extra $1.50 for shipping.

• Bulk discounts are available on orders of five or more. Contact Longview for information.

Send order to: Longview Publishing, 29 Kinderhook Street, Chatham, New York, 12037-1215, USA.